BIOGRAPHICAL NOTE

Mr. Holmes has been asked to supply data for a biographical sketch. He replies that his biography will be found in his Travelogues, each being a chapter from his life of travel.

Elias Burton Holmes was born in January, 1870, in Chicago. In 1883 he became interested in photography, devoting much time to picture-making in the course of his earlier travels in the United States, Cuba, and Mexico. In 1886 he made his first European tour. In 1890 a second and longer tour of England and the Continent gave him the material for his first lecture, "Through Europe with a Camera," which he presented, as an amateur, before the members of the Chicago Camera Club. In 1893 he made his first professional appearance, presenting "Japan—The Country," and "Japan—The Cities," at the Recital Hall of the Auditorium, Chicago, then introducing illustrations all in color for the first time in connection with travel lectures.

During the five following years the Burton Holmes lectures won increasing recognition in the cities of the Middle West. In 1897-98 Mr. Holmes established courses in the larger Eastern cities, then introducing Motion Pictures for the first time. In 1904 he appeared in England, lecturing on American scenic subjects at Queen's Hall, in London, then using the word "Travelogues" to describe his entertainments. He now appears annually in New York, Brooklyn, Boston, Philadelphia, Washington, Pittsburgh, Chicago, Milwaukee, Saint Louis, and San Francisco, giving from ten to twenty performances in each city, presenting five new subjects every season.

In spite of the increasing demands upon his time for platform work, Mr. Holmes continues to devote from five to eight months of the year to travel and the preparation of his Travelogues.

BURTON HOLMES
TRAVELOGUES

With Illustrations from Photographs
By the Author

~ VOLUME ONE ~

THE MCCLURE COMPANY
NEW YORK
MCMX

PRESS OF
EATON & MAINS
NEW YORK

Photo by Lillian Baynes Griffin

TO
MY
THREE

FOREWORD

"To Travel is to Possess the World"

In the foreword to the First Edition of the Travelogues I took occasion to express my gratitude to the lecture-going public who, by their generous support given to the platform presentations of the Travelogues, made possible for me the journeys described in these ten volumes. I have now a new public to thank—the reading public—and to my readers I wish now to express my sincere gratitude for the favor with which they have received the Travelogues as they appear between the covers of these books.

It is difficult for one who, for nearly twenty years, has been traveling as a "deputy sightseer" for so many auditors and readers, not to feel that throughout all these long, busy, interesting years, he has had the best of the bargain. But I am encouraged to believe that the return I bring is fair and just exchange for the wander-privilege that I enjoy, and to believe as well, that not a little of the pleasure that I find in travel is shared by those for whom and by whose favor I travel and thereby "possess the world." I ask nothing better than to be permitted to continue the work which, begun as a labor of love, has now become both a vocation and an avocation.

I wish again to acknowledge the debt of gratitude I owe to my fellow-workers, whose efforts have contributed in so large a measure to the success of the Travelogues: To Katherine Gordon Breed, who was the first to realize the possibilities of the art of coloring lantern slides; to Helen E. Stevenson, to whose exquisite skill and artistic discrimination are due the color-beauty and the convincing truthfulness of the illustrations of all the later Travelogues; to Oscar Bennett Depue, who, since our first lecture, in 1890, has operated the projecting instruments with unfailing accuracy and skill—who since the introduction of Motion Pictures, in 1897, has devoted himself to the perfecting of the art of Cinematography, and who has been for many years and in many lands the ever helpful companion of my travels, and to Louis Francis Brown, who, with business ability and tact, has directed the public presentations of the Travelogues.   E. Burton Holmes.

Honolulu, March 4, 1908.

INTO MOROCCO

INTO MOROCCO

THE transatlantic steamers, that every season bear so many of our fellow-countrymen from our own shores directly to the ports of Italy, pass, as all travelers know, through the Gibraltar Straits. Those who have sailed this course undoubtedly recall with a thrill of pleasure the morning when, after eight days upon the broad Atlantic, they waked to find on either hand the shores of a great continent,—the hills of Spain upon the north, and opposite, the grim forbidding mountains of Morocco.

They will recall, as well, those two gigantic rocky promontories which guard the western entrance to the Mediterranean, — those historic Pillars of Hercules called by the ancients Calpe

and Abyla,— the rocks that for the men of that time marked
the extreme western boundary of the known world.

For centuries Calpe and Abyla, sea-girt mountains torn
asunder by some god of might, were looked upon as the very
ends of the earth.   Beyond them no man dared venture.

Calpe is now the famous fortress of Gibraltar, a bit of
Spain held by the British Empire.   Abyla, upon the shore of
Africa, is now the penal colony Ceuta, a piece
of Moorish territory, con-
quered and held by force of
Spanish a r m s.   At
the bases of these
two mighty cliffs the
waters of two oceans
mingle ; for there the wide
Atlantic, the waterway of

GIBRALTAR

the new world, touches the historic inland ocean, around the
shores of which are grouped the nations that have ruled the
world in ages past.   The narrow channel that links the seas
together serves also to separate two lands so widely dissimilar
that nowhere in the world may the traveler, with so little
effort, enjoy a greater shock of contrast than by crossing the
Gibraltar Strait from Southern Spain to Tangier, in Morocco.

In the space of a few short hours he may there go back a
thousand years ; pass from to-day to a mysterious yesterday,
strangely remote from us in life and thought.   Within sight
of the shores of Europe, within sight of the Spanish railway
stations, within sound of the cannon of Gibraltar, he will
find a land in which there are no roads of any sort, a people
who still use in war the picturesque Arabian flintlock and
the clumsy yataghan ; he will find a remnant of the Middle
Ages, so perfectly preserved by the peculiar embalming influence of the Mohammedan religion that the Morocco of to-
day differs little from the Morocco of the year one thousand.

CAPE SPARTEL LIGHT

One of the most keenly relished moments of my life was the moment when that tiny patch of white, at first so like a drift of snow on the distant Moorish hills, finally resolved itself into a city of strange African aspect, and our ship dropped anchor in what the Moors are pleased to call the *harbor* of Tangier. At last we are about to touch the shore of the strangest, most inaccessible, and most mysterious land

A CITY LIKE A DRIFT OF SNOW

that borders on the Mediterranean. Algeria and Tunis have been modernized by France; railways transport pilgrims to and from the Holy Sepulcher in Palestine; Egypt is but an Anglo-Saxon playground; Greece also has her roads of steel, her daily papers, and her parliament. But Morocco remains unique. Isolated from the world of to-day, and — thanks to that isolation — completely independent, the Empire of the Moorish Sultan has preserved the customs and traditions

CORSAIRS OF TO-DAY

of its past, untouched by modern civilization, unchanged by European influence. The land is to-day as it was, and as it shall be —at least until it be conquered by the infidel, and the throne of the descendants of the Prophet be overthrown by the enemies of Allah.

Meantime, the contemporary devotees of Allah have taken cognizance of our arrival. Lighters are quickly manned, and we are treated to an excellent representation of the manner in which Christian ships were boarded and

PIRATES OR PORTERS?

pillaged by Barbary pirates, in the day when the Corsairs ruled the sea, and all Christendom paid forced tribute to the Sultans, Deys, and Bashas of the Barbary States. A horde of turbaned porters and guides overrun the decks, seize indiscriminately all visible handbags, bundles, and boxes, and toss them, yelling madly all the while, into the boats which rise and fall alongside as the huge swells from the Atlantic glide swiftly underneath our ship. Emulating wise and pious Moslems, we decide to trust in

A RISE IN BEEF

Allah for the recovery of our belongings in due time; and, while the battle of the baggage rages, we turn our attention to a neighboring cattle-ship, where the embarkation of its bovine passengers is proceeding with much celerity and considerable discomfort to the unhappy creatures. The horns of each steer are bound with rope; a hook descends, is engaged in the loops; the donkey-engine snorts, and skyward go the astonished steers, two at a time, in attitudes painfully undignified. But painful as is this rise in beef, the worst is still

A TAIL OF WOE

to come.   To land the animal in the proper place upon the deck, fearless Arabs seize his tail, and by a series of vigorous yanks and twists cause the suffering creature to alight with his nose pointed toward the pen in which he may leisurely re-adjust his elongated carcass, recover from his undisguised indignation, and c o n s o l e himself by watching the precipitate arrival of some other steer   with   whom he may have   had   unfriendly   rela-tions on the Moorish plains.   Thus it is that hundreds of head of Moorish cattle begin their fatal voyage across the strait ; for vast quantities of Moroccan beef go to feed the lean and hungry Spaniard, or to supply the brawn and muscle of Gibraltar's sturdy English garrison.

Having witnessed the acme of this cruelty, we observe with comparative unconcern the unceremonious manner in

PERSUASIVE METHODS

which the animals are persuaded to enter the lighters. A yelling band of Arabs and negroes boost and shove the resisting brute up the gangplank and tumble him head foremost into an already crowded boat, where he regains his feet as best he may. The thuds of falling bodies, the wild cries of the savage workers, continue until, the cargo complete, the craft puts off.

THE BEACH

Looking around we find that we have neared the beach, above which rise the frowning walls of old Tangier. Formerly all passengers landed on the beach, and in rough weather the arrival of a tourist party was a diverting spectacle, the frightened passengers being carried from the tossing rowboats to the sandy beach upon the broad backs of native porters. These porters are invariably Jews, for we are given to understand that no self-respecting Moslem would bend his back to so vile a burden as the carcass of a "Christian dog." We almost regret the tameness of our own arrival, for, thanks to a comparatively calm sea, our boats are able to approach the little pier, and to land us without danger or discomfort save that occasioned by the pressing curiosity of the crowd assembled to watch the coming of the money-spending infidel.

The pier, by the way, represents the one harbor-improvement grudgingly executed by the Moors. The harbor of Tangier could be made most secure at small expense, but the Moors prefer not to tamper with it. "God made it so," they tell us; "we would not presume to altar the wise arrangements of the Almighty." They did not even attempt to repair the old breakwater built by the English years ago and blown up by them upon the close of the brief British occupation. The mention of a British occupation recalls a bit of history. Tangier was taken by the Portuguese in 1471. By them it was held until a Portuguese princess, Catarina of Braganza, went to England as the bride of Charles the Second. She brought to him a splendid dower, including two then

THE PIER

THE HARBOR OF TANGIER

unimportant pieces of real estate,—the island of Bombay in far-off India, and this city of Tangier at the Mediterranean's western gate. Strange indeed the fate of these two bits of real estate. Bombay, the hopeless, far-away possession, became in time the glorious Indian Empire. Tangier, with its unrivaled situation at one of the great doorways of the western world, was held for twenty years, and then, through sheer stupidity, abandoned to barbarism. It was returned by England to the Moors as a free gift; a transaction almost unique in Britain's history. But we must not forget that Gibraltar was not yet a cushion for the British lion's paw; had it been so, another paw would have rested firmly on this Moorish shore, insuring to England absolute control of the Gibraltar Strait.

But if the Anglo-Saxon armies long since relinquished this invaluable prize, the Anglo-Saxon tourist has made Tangier his own. Having passed the solemn Moors who sit at the water-gate at receipt of custom, we find ourselves in a trough-like passage above which rises that stronghold of the globe-trotter, the Continental Hotel. It appears like a huge grin upon the frowning face of the walled city; and its hospitable and cheery aspect contradicts the hostile impression produced by the cannon on the ramparts and the scowling looks of some of the inhabitants.

Let not the tourist be disappointed because a modern structure first obtrudes itself. Tangier is not the real Morocco; it is a Moslem seaport, defiled by contact with an infidel world.

THE CONTINENTAL HOTEL

The late Sultan of Morocco disowned the city. When last he came and beheld the changes wrought by foreigners, it is said that he exclaimed: "Allah confound these greedy Christians!—they have stolen from me my beautiful Tangier!"

The crowd we see near yonder doorway is gathered by a distribution of pennies to the poor, —

THE MAIN STREET OF TANGIER

an act of charity performed every week by the officials of
the custom-house.   How superbly important seems the white
robed Moor charged with the graceful task of pressing into
every outstretched dirty palm a shining Spanish copper worth
about two cents, while his assistant keeps his eyes well open
to detect repeaters.   Every now and then there is a lively
row, resulting from the detection of some clever unfortunate,

A CROWD OF MENDICANTS

who has changed rags with a fellow
pauper, and has complacently applied for a second dose of
governmental generosity.   Utter poverty and black misery
are depicted upon the rags and visages of the expectant
throng—even the babies wear oldish, knowing expressions
on their little faces.   A strange feature is the curious little
pigtail worn by the boys,—a pigtail growing all awry, sprout-
ing, not from the crown, but from one side of the head.
The pigtail is an agent of salvation; on it depends the

hope of heaven;
for we are told
that at the day
of judgment
Allah is to lift
the righteous
faithful by their
pigtails into
paradise. Apro-
pos of this state-
ment and other
statements heard
in the course of
our journey, it

PENNIES FOR THE POOR

may be well to quote an Arab maxim: "Never believe all
you hear; for he who believes all he hears often will believe
that which is not." Another maxim from the same source
contains excellent advice for the traveler, and much comfort
for the lazy: "Do not do all that you can; for he who does
all he can, often will do that which he should not." Another
is a pearl of great price to the returned traveler especially:
"Do not say all you know; for he who says all he knows
often will say that which he knows not." There is yet a
fourth gem of Arabian wisdom with a similar setting: "Do
not spend all you have; for
he who spends all he hath,
often will spend that which
he hath not."

AFTER
TASTING
GOVERNMENTAL
GENEROSITY

The arrival in Tangier is
unlike that in any other city
in the world. Every native
face is a type, every group a
picture. We begin to
love the dirt, the smells

(not all bad ones, by any means, merely strange foreign smells suggestive of what is old and Oriental), and as we make our way into the perplexing maze of Tangier's weird little alleys, we seem to have taken a journey backward through the ages. Our sensations might be those of one suddenly transported from this familiar earth to a strange planet; and yet the hills of Spain are seen across the straits. A group of water-carriers earnestly discussing some important piece of news that probably will never be published to the Christian world, forms a picture almost Biblical in its antiquity. They are retailers of that precious beverage,—the beverage of all the worshipers of Allah,—the true gift

COMRADES IN POVERTY of God, pure water. We can forgive the Moslem many things, because he never has been, and, so long as he clings to the religion of his fathers, never will be, a drunkard. The water-bags are goat-skins, the long neck serving as a faucet; but although we are as thirsty as the African sun itself, we do not patronize these itinerant fountains; being newly come to Tangier, our squeamishness interferes with an indulgence in many little comforts; but what a surprising revolution will be worked by an expedition into Morocco! We shall return from the interior with adamantine sensibilities as regards such trifles. But to-day we are open to impressions of all kinds. So

dazed are we by the strangeness of our surroundings that we
have left no words with which to express our delight when,
stepping out at last upon the balcony of our hotel, we look
down upon Tangier, the "White City of the Straits." Below
us is the beach, dotted with the rude camps of pilgrims who
are awaiting ships for Mecca; above it are tiers of batteries;
beyond we see a mass of white cubes, the dwelling-houses of

WATER CARRIERS

the Moors. A dainty minaret, green-tiled
and graceful, rises from this angular snow-bank; near it, the
flags of foreign nations float above their respective consulates
and legations. Strange indeed this mingling of the Occidental and the Oriental, beautiful indeed this city of Tangier,
the sentinel city of Morocco, posted here at the corner of
Africa to watch with jealous eyes for the coming of the
inevitable conqueror who is to sally forth from the gates of
Christendom, dimly discerned across the Gibraltar Channel.
Of small account will be these batteries, furnished with anti-

TANGIER

quated cannon. These crippled dogs of war rend nothing
more tangible than air, and damage nothing but ear-drums.
And frequently is the air rent, and the ear assaulted, for the
arrival of every man-of-war is greeted with a ferocious salvo
of artillery, at sound of which the Moors gaze proudly seaward, expand their chests, recall the days when Moorish
corsairs ruled the seas, and dream of future victories for the
armies of the Prophet.

The sunshine in this land is wonderful; at seven in the
morning it is so brilliant that we cannot bear the reflection
from the chalky housetops, and recover the use of our eye-
sight only when in the dark and narrow corridors that serve
the Tangerines in lieu of streets. The thoroughfare which
every visitor must traverse when going from the hotel to the
great or lesser market-places, is distinctly banal in aspect.
It is the leading shopping street of the European resi-

THE WHITE CITY OF THE STRAITS

THE STREET OF EUROPEAN SHOPS

dents; its shops are stuffed with canned provisions, patent-medicines, and playing-cards, while a saloon or two make known their presence, even to the blind, by strong gin-like aromas wafted thence. When lost in the labyrinthine maze of Moorish Tangier, the foreigner has but to follow his nose to reach the place where rum and brandy are on sale, and European civilization well in evidence. Then he may emerge into the lesser market-place, or "Soko," as it is called in local speech. Here he finds one tiny French café and the postal stations of England, Spain, and France; for as Morocco's postal-service is on a par with its other governmental enterprises, these nations each maintain post-offices in Tangier and an elaborate courier service in the interior. European mails now penetrate to Fez, even to Mequinez and Morocco City, with tolerable dispatch and certainty.

While we refresh ourselves at the café, we are amused by the ape-like antics of a negro from the far-away province of Suss. His wig of wool is hung with shells and teeth and nails, all of which clatter as he dances to the music of a pair of iron castanets.

But he cannot compare in picturesqueness with this other visitor—a superb representative of the saintly beggar class. So imposing a revelation of dignity in rags it is not possible to find among men of any other race or creed. We learn that this haughty mendicant is crazy; that in Morocco, insanity is the most valuable asset of those who desire to engage in what European residents irreverently term the "saint business." The Moors are convinced that if the mind of a man inhabit not his body, it is because God, having discerned in that mind much beauty of holiness, retains it in paradise as a thing too precious to be sent with the man to earth. Therefore great consideration should be shown for the mortal coil   pertaining to

THE CAFE IN THE LITTLE SOKO

that mind. Thus "crazy" has become a synonym for
"sanctified," and an insane man has but to mumble prayers,
and watch his saner fellow-citizens vie with one another in
propitiating him with gifts and offerings. But sometimes
this insanity is only feigned, and some of these weird charac-
ters are in reality agents of the militant Moslem brotherhoods
of Tripoli and Tunis, charged with the spreading of a
Mohammedan propaganda and the keeping alive of bitter
anti-Christian agitation.

If we follow this splendid *misérable*, we shall presently lose sight of him in the confusion of the be-draped,
be-hooded crowd surging through the upper gate that opens
toward the greater market-place, or "Soko," on the high
ground behind the city. The women are closely veiled
and buried in the   smothering folds
of the white   w o o l e n
"haik."   All rich

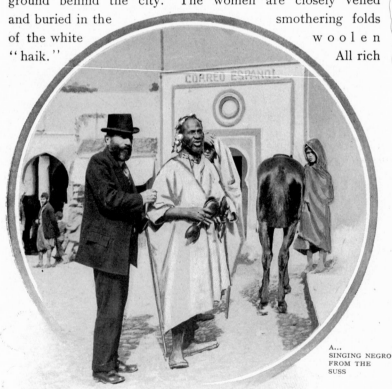

A...
SINGING NEGRO
FROM THE
SUSS

DIGNITY IN RAGS

men wear the colored caftan, or the white burnoose, and some are draped in muslin veils ; the poor men wear the rough brown jelaba, a sack-like garment with a pointed hood. On feet that are not bare are yellow slippers ; on the heads, a red fez, a white turban, or a monkish-looking hood.

The Soko on Thursday or on Sunday (local market-days) is a sight to be remembered. The market-place itself is, literally, out of sight ; during the night and early morning, living things, from men to mules, from women to camels, and things inanimate, from eggs to beef and mutton, from oats to olive oil, have been gathered together, spread out, heaped up, forming a mass that moves and gives forth cries and odors. Twice every week the sun looks down upon a scene like this. Here in the Soko is the true frontier between the Christian and the Moslem worlds. Here is the border-land of the real Africa ; here couriers from Fez and from the desert region farther south meet the postmen of the European

services; here surges the murky tide
of African humanity ; here breaks the
last sun-crested wave of continental
civilization ; here top-hats and turbans
mingle ; here Europe ends
and Africa begins.

From the windows of
the legation of a European
nation which open upon
the Soko, there are wafted
lively measures of piano
melody ; and these are almost drowned by the prayers
of beggars, the vociferations
of the trading throng, and

A SPLENDID " MISÉRABLE "

the incantations of half-crazy conjurors.   Conquering our first
emotion of aversion, almost of fear, we press through the ill-
smelling, yelling crowd, and work our way to the front rank

THE BE-DRAPED, BE-HOODED CROWD

THE BORDERLAND OF THE REAL AFRICA

of a magician's audience. The conjuror welcomes us with
curses, and refuses to continue his performance until our

Photograph by Nelson Ludington Barnes   THE SOKO ON SUNDAY

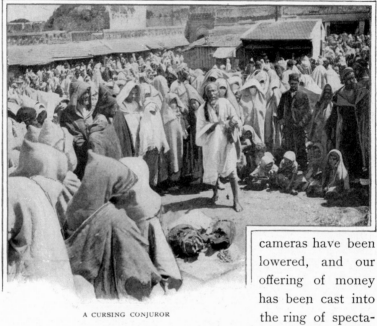

A CURSING CONJUROR

cameras have been lowered, and our offering of money has been cast into the ring of specta-tors.   Then, muttering strange prayers, he gathers from the ground a handful of straw, calls on his god, and on the gen-erosity of the onlookers, and blowing upon the straw causes it miraculously to burst into flames, which instantly consume it.   More offerings are then demanded, more prayers are said, and more unflattering remarks are made concerning us ; for to curse and to insult a Christian is a pious deed.   Another trick is performed : A youth is (supposedly) hypnotized, and while he seems unconscious, a long bodkin is thrust through the flesh of his throat and the ends left protruding, while the old fakir takes up the most successful collection of the afternoon. Because we do not give more silver coins instead of Moorish coppers, the holy wonder-worker exhausts his stock of anti-Christian expletives, much to the edification of his sympa-thetic congregation.   So great is the hatred of Christians on the part of the lower classes that even the beggars return

"MAY ALLAH BURN YOUR GRANDMOTHER!"

HYPNOTIZED!

curses instead of thanks, atoning for the sin of receiving unclean Christian money by calling down the wrath of heaven, not only upon our heads, but also upon the heads of all who are dear to us, or related to us, even unto the fourth and fifth generation of those who have preceded us and are responsible for our existence. One simple and popular anathema is, "May Allah burn your grandmother!" Another expresses the wish that the wife of your great-grandfather may enjoy perpetual torridity in the nether world.

The blind mendicants beg in little companies of six or eight. One sightless horrible, standing, cries aloud for charity in the name of his companions. These are not pleasant sights, but no true impression of Tangier can be imparted if we leave out of the picture the rags, the beggars, and the dirt.   One more sad spectacle must suffice — that of an old beggar, shriveled by age, baked by the cruel sun, bent beneath the burden of many hopeless years, not even clad in rags, but merely covered with a mat of straw — a superlative expression of Moroccan misery.

Here we may recall the story of the English clergyman, who, touched at the sight of all this misery and ignorance, resolved to tell the gospel-story to the people of Tangier — to make a public exhortation in the market-place.   With the greatest difficulty he secured a capable interpreter, for most of the hotel guides feared to assist him in his rash and dangerous crusade.   When the pious preacher began his sermon in the market-place, he was not only surprised, but thoroughly delighted at the reverence with which his glowing   words, translated by

A PETTY TRANSACTION

MOROCCAN
MISERY

his guide, were received by the atten-
tive throng of Moslems.   When he had
finished, he was even urged to speak
again.   Undoubtedly the good man carried away a soul filled with joy
because of the good seed he had
planted here.   One English news-
paper   chronicled   the   marked
interest shown by the heathen in
the words of Christian truth ; but
it is to be hoped that the good
man will never learn that while
he stood in the center of this meeting place and spoke, his
diplomatic interpreter and guide not only held the respectful
ears of the crowd, but possibly saved the missionary's life
by cleverly turning the orthodox sermon into one of the
favorite romances from the "Arabian Nights."

No, it is virtually impossible to turn the Moslem from the
faith of his fathers.   His religion forms too intimate a part of

A SYNDICATE OF BLIND BEGGARS

his daily life ; his religious fasts and festivals are observed
with a strictness that is absolute.   We chanced to witness
the celebration of the great feast called Aid-el-Kebir.   The
early morning finds us on a hillside near the market, where
there is gathered a multitude of spectral forms.   Here the
slanting rays of the newly risen sun draw out all shadows to
a grotesque length, while from the midst of the assemblage

MOSLEM SALVATIONISTS

there bursts a cloud of smoke which like a veil conceals
the wild tribesmen who are there performing a fantastic
powder-play with old-fashioned noisy flintlocks.   An hour
later the populace repairs to the high-walled garden of a
suburban mosque to witness the sacrifice of a magnificent
ram.   The ram, however, is not allowed to die in peace, for
according to an ancient custom its bleeding body must be
borne swiftly down through the city streets to the great

Photograph by Mr. White, of Tangier

GATHERING TO CELEBRATE THE "GREAT FEAST"

mosque in the lower town, where, if it arrives living, the
omen for the year is pronounced good; if dead, the wise men
shake their heads and prophesy disaster. Hence are the
swiftest runners employed to dash with the dying burden
across the Soko, into the city gates, down abrupt alleys to
the other sanctuary. Like a host of madmen they rush past
us, the sheep slung in a basket dragged by four men. Thrice
do the bearers stumble, thrice is the bleeding mass rolled in
the dust, thrice is the mad race resumed, the people urging
on the panting runners with cries, and sticks, and stones.
The sacrificial ram is dead upon arriving at the mosque, yet
it is given out by the authorities that it was still alive. The

NEAR THE SUBURBAN MOSQUE

THE BASHA OF TANGIER

disorderly mob disappears through the arched portals of the
town, and a dignified procession crosses the Soko. The
Basha, or Governor, of the province of Tangier, with his
mounted escort, is returning from the recent ceremony.
Although his salary is only seventy-five dollars a month, this
wise official, by strict economy, has grown very rich. He,
like all the swells, rides a handsome mule; for in Morocco
mules enjoy much favor and are preferred to horses for long
journeys and for city promenades; in fact, for everything,
save battle.

A feast is held in every house upon this sacred day, a
sheep being sacrificed for each adult member of the family.

We see many a woolly burden carried
through the streets upon the shoulders
of the purchaser.   Other means also are
employed for the successful home-bring-
ing of the fatted creatures.   One man
will attempt to drag the balky ram by the
horns; another, more clever, will seize the
hind feet and shove the sheep along as one
would push a wheelbarrow, the result being a
wildly zigzag progress down the steep, narrow
streets. Throughout the entire Moslem world
this day of Aid-el-Kebir is celebrated.   At
Mecca, the fountain-head of the Moslem faith,
a hundred and twenty thousand sheep are put
to the knife at each recurrence of the festival.
Even in Tangier the feast may be likened to

THE SACRIFICIAL RAM

an ovine Saint Bartholomew Massacre, a day as fatal to these
woolly victims as is Thanksgiving day to the devoted gobblers
of New England.   The city becomes a mammoth butcher-
shop; the gutters in the narrow streets run red with blood.
To escape these little tragedies, we make our way up to the
higher regions of the town, where the Palace of the
Governor, the Treasury Building, and the Prison are
found in close proximity to one another.   We
find the palace inaccessible, the treasury empty,
and the prison full.

The prison externally is a blank,
white structure, high and in sad want
of repair.   We enter a small vestibule,
where several lazy guards
are stationed; they indicate
an opening in the wall, a
window, protected by heavy
bars and closed by a thick

AN OVINE SAINT BARTHOLOMEW

metal shutter. This, they say, is the unique means of ingress to the prison. No means of egress is required, for prisoners seldom come thence alive. A hasty glance through a round hole in the metal shutter reveals a filthy, spacious hall, crowded with animated mummies loosely wrapped in earth-colored tatters. We are told that no food is furnished to the prisoners save that which may be brought by pitying

THE ONLY DOORWAY TO THE PRISON

outsiders, friends of the unfortunates within. The government allows its victims the one privilege of reaching out through the little aperture for the bread of pity. Some of the prisoners make colored baskets, like those which hang upon the wall, and eke out an existence by the sale of these. The presence of a traveler becoming known in the den, baskets by the dozen come tumbling out to tempt him in charity to buy.

While it is difficult for a man to get out of the prison, it is absolutely impossible for a man to enter the harem of the

THE PRISON

THE BASHA'S PALACE AND THE TREASURY

neighboring palace of the
Basha; but foreign women are sometimes presented to the
Basha's wives. One feminine visitor reports that the mysterious beauties examined carefully the details of her dress.
" Oh, " said one to another, as she discovered that the white
hands were gloved, " see! — the American lady has two skins
upon her hands!" In reply to a question as to what little
present might be welcome, one Oriental matron replied with
much enthusiasm, " Ah, send us from your country some
of those pretty little combs with the fine teeth — they are so
much more useful than our coarse ones, and — we need them
very much!"

Leaving the inhospitable palace, we descend to the one
building of all Tangier, in which we are certain to receive a cordial welcome. The shield of the United States Consulate-General dispels the Moorish gloom of at least one dim thoroughfare.
Here in this land of despotism and darkness it shines forth
like a symbol of liberty and light. The Consul-General, Dr.

AT THE U. S. CONSULATE-GENERAL

J. J. Barclay, tells us with justifiable pride that his grandfather, the Hon. Thos. Barclay, negotiated the first treaty between the United States and the Empire of Morocco. He shows us two interesting documents; one, the Consular Commission signed by George Washington; the other, the Exequatur granted by the Sultan to the first Consul of the young American Republic. The following is a translation of the Exequatur, made by the official interpreter of the Consulate - General:

"In the name of God, the Clement and Merciful. There is no strength or force but in God, the High and Eternal. From Abdallah Mohammed, Ben Abdallah, in whom the Almighty deposited his confidence."

IMPERIAL SEAL

"To the great President of the American States: I salute you with empressment, and hope in God you are well. The Ambassador, Thomas Barclay, has come to us bearing a precious letter from the Spaniard Charles. We have read it, and

we understand all its contents in which you asked us peace
with you like the other Christian nations with whom you have
made peace. We accept your demand, and peace be between
us on land and sea, and according to the Treaties you demanded
from us. We have written this in our letter to you, to which
I affixed my Sheriffian seal, and we have ordered all our em-
ployees in my seaports to do with your vessels and merchandise
that go to my seaports, as they do with those of the Spaniards,
and your vessels can enter, and anchor with safety in any of
my seaports you choose, from Tetuan to Wadnoon; they can
also buy and sell, and do business for themselves, and they
can depart. We have answered just like this to the great
Spaniard Charles, who wrote me a letter on your behalf. I
join with you in perfect peace and friendship. In peace.

"This is written the first day of the blessed month of
Ramadan 1200 (1785–1786)."

THE HOME OF MR. PERDICARIS

To Dr. Barclay we confided our cherished plans for a journey into Morocco, and asked him to advise, assist, and guide us. He became most zealous in our cause; made light of the difficulty and danger said to attend the journey, spoke in glowing terms of the pleasures and surprises in store for us. Within the week all the formalities incident to our departure are complied with. The Moorish Minister of Foreign Affairs has graciously granted us permission to traverse the Empire of his Master, the Sultan of Morocco, and he has provided us with letters to many provincial chiefs, and to the Governor of Fez, the capital. He has promised us a military escort equal to our needs, and has called down blessings upon us, and has accepted the usual little token of our high esteem in the form of a pile of Spanish dollars. All this we owed to the good offices of Dr. Barclay, to whom also we owed

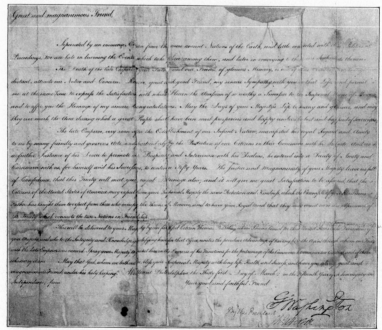

COMMISSION OF CONSUL THOMAS BARCLAY SIGNED BY GEORGE WASHINGTON

a delightful glimpse of the gay social life led by the foreign residents and diplomats in old Tangier.

The hillsides round about the city are dotted with luxurious, palatial villas, in the drawing-rooms of which cosmopolitan gatherings dis-cuss the latest continental news in half a dozen languages. Ac-cording to an English dictum, "Society in Tan-gier is split into

EXEQUATUR OF THE FIRST U. S. CONSUL TO TANGIER

three factions, — those who will know one another, those who won't know one another, and those who must know one another, but don't like to." There are artists, musicians, and diplomats, millionaires and globe-trotters, and ex-consuls and ex-ministers by the dozen; for they say that when one has lived in Tangier, it is not pos-sible to be contented elsewhere. Therefore many men who come hither for a few years of diplomatic service, end by purchasing hillside villas and becoming permanent residents.

A LAST LOOK AT TANGIER

Tangerine hospitality is famous for its freedom, but we have little time for social dissipations. Every moment is occupied in preparations for departure. A few days more and we are to leave this most attractive corner of Cosmopolis, bid farewell to friends, to comfort, and to civilization. The hotel will give place to the tent, the daily pony-canter on the beach to the long weary marches of our caravan over hills and mountains, in the region where there are no roads, where to-day is the same as yesterday. We are to voyage forth upon a strange expanse, where the ship of Moorish civilization, stranded upon the shoals of the religion of immutability, has lain rotting since the conquest of Granada.

It is but right that you should know something about the men upon whom our future comfort, welfare, and safety entirely depend. Let me introduce, first of all, the most faithful of guides, the most honest of dragomans, the cheeriest of companions, the cleverest of pathfinders, the best of cooks, and — the most amusing prevaricator I have ever known. His name is like all Moorish names, a mouthful, "Haj Abd-er-Rahman Salama." We see him first at the door of his dwelling, a bright young Salama at his side. We speak with him in French and Spanish, for his much-advertised command of English is monumentally inadequate. Moreover in French he speaks like a gentleman, in English like a blackguard; one language having been learned in Algiers and in Paris, the other picked up from profane sportsmen, while serving as dragoman for pig-sticking expeditions. As for his name, we forget it altogether, and address him simply as Haj, the word " Haj" being a sort of honorific prefix, meaning Pilgrim, in other words, a righteous Moslem who has made the Holy Pilgrimage to Mecca. When it was noised abroad that we were thinking of a trip to Fez, the professional guides of Tangier looked on us as lawful, tempting prey. One Jewish pathfinder proffered his services and outfit for seven English pounds a day. Then others came with other propositions, and there ensued a veritable rate-war in which tents figure in place of Pullman cars, and, in place of sixty-miles-an-hour locomotives, mules that travel only sixteen miles a day. And Haj triumphed over all competitors, not because he made the lowest bid, but because we saw in him a useful, clever man, full of resource, one of the few Moorish minds able to respond to Anglo-Saxon sympathies. He is one who has bridged the gulf between the Moslem and the Christian races, at the cost, possibly, of his orthodoxy and his hopes of heaven.

In violent contrast to him in these respects, is our military escort: our fighting-force, assigned us by the government and consisting of one personal

THE BEST OF GUIDES,
HAJ ABD-ER-RAHMAN SALAMA

KAID LHARBI, OUR MILITARY ESCORT

unit — with dignity and bigotry and decorative picturesqueness enough for half a regiment. Kaid Lharbi, for such are his title and name, belongs to the Makhazni, or corps of irregular cavalry, the most ornamental branch of the Moorish Sultan's army. No traveler is permitted to go into Morocco unless chaperoned by a Makhazni. Kaid Lharbi will be for us a sort of living passport, his presence at the head of our caravan assuring all persons that we are traveling under the protection of the Moorish government, and that offenses against us will be severely punished. Without this living token of governmental sanction for our expedition, it would be within the power of any local chief to arrest our progress, sending us back in ignominious captivity to Tangier ; or, if he preferred, he could rob us with impunity. Kaid Lharbi is therefore a valuable acquisition from the standpoints both of safety and of picturesqueness. He is Moorish in the fullest sense; he thinks such thoughts and dreams such dreams as did his fathers half a thousand years ago. He carries a flintlock made in Tetuan, and is supplied with a lump of lead and a small bullet-mold, that in case of attack he may be able to cast the necessary bullets.

The sixth day of May is appointed for the departure of our caravan. It is a memorable day for us, because it marks the close of a long period of doubt and uncertainty as to the possibility of undertaking the expedition, and because it marks the beginning of a new life — the entry into a new world, which is yet immeasurably old. The pack-mules in charge of the three servants have been sent on ahead to await us in the suburbs. Kaid Lharbi, muffled in his blue burnoose, has been stationed like an equestrian statue at the door of the hotel since early morning. Haj, the guide, is here, there, and everywhere, attending to the thousand and one little details and difficulties that always arise at the last moment.

We bid adieu to our acquaintances at the hotel door. At last the start is made, we file through narrow streets, cross the crowded market-place, and on its outskirts overtake the pack-mules and the muleteers. A few necessary articles, brought at the last moment by our thoughtful Haj, who would have felt himself disgraced had he forgotten anything, are added to the already heavy burdens of the mules.

THE DEPARTURE

Then at a signal, our men, the skeptic Haj, and all the
rest reverently turn their faces toward the East, toward
Holy Mecca,   while Kaid Lharbi, his

ADDING THE LAST
ITEM TO THE PACKS

head bent low over his horse's neck, intones an impressive
prayer for the successful and happy termination of our
journey. This pious duty done, the order for a forward
march is given, and in single file our little train of men,
horses, mules, and donkeys winds its way out of Tangier,
every hoof-beat of the animals taking us nearer to the
Middle Ages. Gradually the suburban street becomes a
lane, gradually the lane fades away, becoming a mere trail,
and finally the trail itself, crossing a ruined bridge, loses
itself in the roadless vastness of the Moorish Empire.

Never in all my travels have I more keenly felt that
oppressive sense of separation from things known and familiar than at this moment. No previous departure by train or

steamer had ever seemed so definitely to break the link that
binds us to our own age and our own civilization. Here, at
the bridge that spans a dry and thirsty river-bed, all semblance of civilization abruptly terminates ; before us lies a
land without railways, without roads, without fences, hedges,
trees — without dividing lines of any kind, save long low
ranges of barren hills and, in the eastern distance, the crests
of savage mountains. Across this roadless empire we are
now to travel for many days ; overhead there will hang at
times a scorching sun, at times dark storm-clouds are to form
our canopy ; around us is to stretch a savage, silent land.
Before us lies a scarcely distinguishable track, worn by the
hoofs of countless caravans in years
that are un- counted. But

THE EDGE OF CIVILIZATION

for me, in
the foreground
of every Moorish landscape looms the figure of Kaid Lharbi.
All day I looked over my horse's ears upon Kaid Lharbi's back,
his horse's tail, and his cloak of blue, his broad-brimmed

5

ACROSS THE
ROADLESS PLAINS

hat, such as are made and worn by the women of Tetuan, its brim so broad that colored cords are required as guy ropes to sustain it. That famous hat served both as a parasol and umbrella; the image of its expansive brim, flapping gaily in the breeze, or drooping gloomily beneath an avalanche of water from the skies, will never be effaced from memory. All day I looked upon that hat; at

" TWO HARD-WORKING HUMBLE SOULS "

night I saw it in my dreams; and, at the journey's end, I acquired it by purchase, and it now hangs upon my wall,—a mute reminder of a memorable ride.

Less picturesquely mounted, less self-important than Kaid Lharbi but far more useful, diligent, and kindly were the two hard-working humble souls who rode on little burros in

" BOKHURMUR "

THE FIRST HALTING PLACE

the rear of the procession. On them devolved the hardest
labors of the journey — to load the mules ; to drive or guide
them all day long, frequently running along for miles on
foot ; to help or urge the struggling, overburdened animals
through the muddy ditches ; to unpack everything at night,
set up the tents, build fires, tether and find forage for nine
animals, including their own patient little donkeys — this
formed their regular daily routine. Yet they are cheerful
with it all, although sun and rain, health and sickness, must
mean the same to them ; they must not rest on pain of being
left behind. Their names, as near as it was possible for us to
grasp them, were respectively, Bokhurmur and Abuktayer,
but which was "Abuktayer," and which "Bokhurmur" is a
point upon which my friend and I could never quite agree.

DEVELOPING OUR CANVAS VILLAGE

At a command from Haj, the caravan has halted.   " We
have arrived," adds Haj ; " unload ! pitch camp ! We are
where we should be at five o'clock."

Here, then, is to be our first camping-ground, here for the
first time we are to see our outfit set up in its entirety ; here
we are, for the first time, to sleep in tents like the Bedouins ;

THE FIRST CAMP

to begin the new life that promises to be so strange and fascinating. With keenest interest we watch our little canvas
village develop.   At first we attempt to aid the men, but Haj
sternly prohibits all effort on our part.   It is not consistent
with our dignity as great American *seigneurs* to stoop to
labor. A mattress is hastily unpacked and spread upon the
ground, and on it we repose in lordly laziness. Had we
driven a single tent-peg, we should have lost completely the
respect of our Oriental hirelings.

Three tents compose the camp : one large green tent of
English manufacture for the grand *seigneurs*, two Moorish
tents, for the accommodation of the faithful suite. One by
one the canvas houses rise.   The animals are tethered close

at hand. From the neighboring village, ragged men bring fodder for the animals, eggs and chickens for the foreign lords. These things, of course, are paid for, because, our expedition not being of a diplomatic or official nature, we do not enjoy the right to be served with the traditional "Mouna," that is, we cannot levy contributions upon the tribes. Our letters of recommendation demand for us merely the protection of the village chiefs. When a great man, be he a native potentate or the ambassador of a foreign nation, passes through the land in state, all things are by the Sultan's command furnished him gratis by the people of each bashalik, or province. As the villagers gather in a silent, curious pyramid, to watch with deepest interest everything we do, to examine with uncomprehending eyes our mysterious camp-

A SILENT, CURIOUS PYRAMID

beds, our folding chairs and tables, let me describe another
custom that is observed during the progress of an official
expedition.

When the people of a village have a boon to ask or a
favor to entreat from the Sultan at Fez, such as the release
from prison of some fellow tribesman, or the recall of some
too cruel tax-extortioner, a deputation of villagers comes in
procession to the tent of the great man, and before the
entrance sacrifices a heifer or a sheep. If the chief or the
ambassador is inclined to grant the petition, or to further
the purposes of the suppliants, he accepts the gift of meat
and it is eaten by his escort. If he denies their request, he
averts his face ; no man is permitted to touch the sacrifice,
and it is left as food for birds of prey.

The camp arrangements being complete, and all things
made ready for our reception, Haj proudly but anxiously
invites our inspection of the interior arrangements of our
canvas home. "Well done, Haj Abd-er-Rahman Salama !"
we exclaim, as a vision of coziness and comfort is revealed
to us. Well done, indeed ! No wanderer in a barbarous
land could ask for more. We
behold soft beds with fresh
white sheets and pillow
cases, bright rugs upon

"WITH
UNCOMPREHENDING EYES"

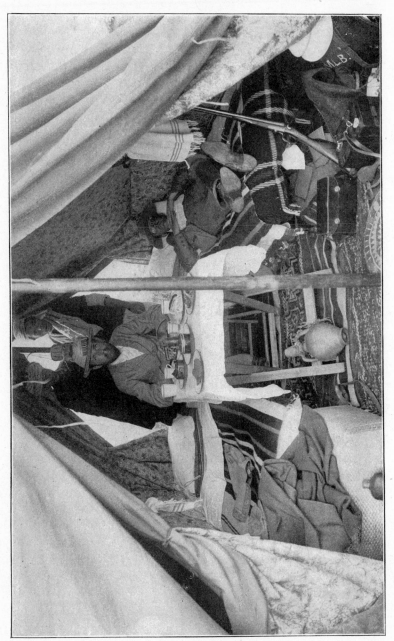

CHEZ NOUS

"HAJ" IN DOUBT

"HAJ" IN JOY

the turf, a table large enough for two, well spread with tempting food, and all this is wholly protected from the heat and cold and rain and wind by a fine triple tent, green without and pink-lined within, just like a luxurious boudoir. And now this is to be our home for forty long delightful days and as many nights. No matter where our camp may happen to lie, on the barren hillside, in the fertile plain, or on the outskirts of a dirty town, this cozy corner will be always the same. No matter how wild and hostile are the surrounding scenes, we have but to draw the tent-flaps close to find ourselves delightfully *chez nous*. And furthermore, we are just as well served as in an excellent hotel, for although we lack the convenient electric-button, yet we have a perfect substitute in the person of Achmedo al Hishu, our valet, groom, and butler. Achmedo is not handsome, but he is indispensable; he is always at hand, answering a call before it is made, satisfying a want as soon as it is felt. He speaks a kind of Tangerine servant language; a mixture of Spanish, French, and English, startling at times, but always comprehensible. His one fault is a fondness for the pipe, in which he smokes — not comparatively innocent

"ACHMEDO"

OUR CANVAS HOUSES

tobacco — but the nerve-deadening weed called "keef."
Moreover, we observe him to be a great imbiber. As he
rides across the plain, proudly seated on the summit of a
baggage-pack (beneath which the poor mule is scarcely
visible), Achmedo may be seen to lift a bottle reverently
to his lips, three times to every mile. We marveled that he
could preserve his equilibrium day after day, until we discovered the nature of the contents of that bottle — cold tea,
flavored with mint and sugar.

A word more about our invaluable Haj Abd-er-Rahman
Salama, whose dusky face reflects the anxiety that fills his
soul as he awaits our verdict upon the first meal prepared
by him. He claimed to be himself a skillful chef, and
insisted that he be allowed to manage the commissary
department without interference. We reluctantly intrusted
our gastronomic welfare to this homely heathen, and throughout the day visions of hard-tack and rancid bacon haunted
our hungry souls. We scarcely dared to hope for better fare,
furnished, as it was to be, by this cunning caterer, who has
us completely in his power. He is free to starve or stuff us ;
no power can touch him now. If he prove faithless, we
must suffer ; we are his slaves for forty days ; he is our

master, we must go whither he leads, for we are in an unknown country ; we must eat that which he provides, for we are in an empty land.

But when dinner is served, we enthusiastically declare that Haj is the best cook south of Paris ; and at this his handsome features are convulsed into a smile of proud and happy satisfaction. The dinner served on that first evening in our camp was a culinary triumph ; a perfect little table d'hote : consommé ; fish, fresh from the basket of a Tangier fisherman ; sweetbread croquettes ; broiled chicken ; salad ; blancmange, cooled in a neighboring stream ; a sip of Turkish coffee, a little glass of benedictine, and then a cigarette. All this prepared and served in a little tent pitched far from town or city in the midst of the somber Moorish plain. How it was possible for Haj to turn out from his tiny canvas kitchen, and with his crude utensils, dishes so varied and delicious, was an enduring mystery to us, but we fared sumptuously throughout the journey. We lived in greater comfort and were better served than in the French hotels of Algeria or the big hotels of Spain, and we dined as well as

OVER THE RED HILL

on the Paris boulevards; and for all this, we paid a price
ridiculously low.   Haj provided the entire outfit, — two
horses, five mules, two donkeys, and three tents; paid wages
to three servants, baksheesh to the military escort, furnished
all provisions, cooked for us, schemed for us, guided us, — all
for twelve dollars daily and a present at the journey's end.
Beyond this small sum we spent not a penny, save for the
purchase of some little souvenirs.

On the second morning, dark, lowering clouds obscure the
heavens; yet, despite the threat of a stormy day we break
camp, a task requiring about two hours of hard labor for our
men.   Our animals are loosed and roam at will, browsing
upon the fresh sweet clover.   The men of the neighboring
village, who have been guarding the camp since evening,
return to their huts at daybreak; all night they sat in groups
around our tents, chanting or mumbling prayers to keep
themselves awake.   We reward them with a present of silver
coins, which they accept with greedy eyes.   At last, the
countless things pertaining to the camp being all stowed
securely in the broad packs, we bid farewell to our first
Morocco halting-place and begin what, we have been told,
will prove the most disagreeable stage of the entire journey —
the crossing of the Red Hill; an
experience dreaded by all
caravans, especially in
rainy weather.   And
rightly unpopular is
it, this trail of

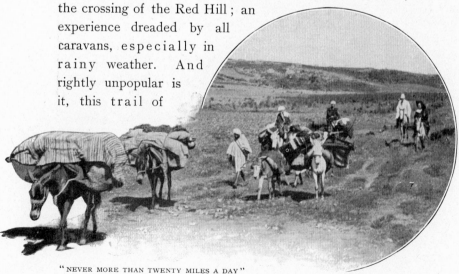

"NEVER MORE THAN TWENTY MILES A DAY"

THE CAMP OF THE GOVERNOR

broken rock and slimy reddish clay, where at every step our horses stumble or slip, where every now and then a pack mule, fixing the forefeet firmly, goes glissading swiftly down the hill, until, over-balanced by its enormous burden, it literally capsizes, and lies helpless in the mire while the crew jettisons the cargo, rights the poor hulk, re-ballasts it, and steers it down the dangerous channel, using the tail as rudder and sharpened sticks as inspiration. Frequent heavy downpours of rain add to our discomfort, drenching us to the skin and threatening to shipwreck our hopes of reaching camp with tents and baggage dry. But suddenly, an hour after we reach the plain, the sky is cleared and swept completely clean, as if a great sponge had wiped away the rain clouds; and then a beaming sun quickly dries men and animals and burdens, causing us to give off clouds of vapor until we can scarcely distinguish one another. And thus we journey on, never faster than at a rapid walk, with frequent delays caused by the breaking of a strap, the balky temper of a mule, or by a deep ditch difficult to ford. We cover never more than twenty miles a day. At midday we come upon the camp of the Basha of Tangier, and near it we make a halt

for luncheon. Haj informs us that the Governor
has come up country to arrange a few official
robberies, and to ad-
minister a little Moor-
ish justice—a peculiar
quality of justice.

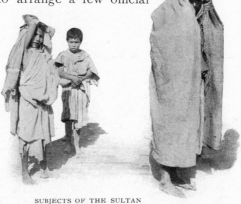

The collection of
taxes is, however, the
Basha's most impor-
tant business. The
taxpayers are assem-
bled around his tent,
and pay in money, in

SUBJECTS OF THE SULTAN

produce, and in cattle. The assessment varies according
to the visible possessions and apparent prosperity of the
victim. No wise subject of the Moorish Sultan ever boasts
of his possessions. All feign poverty; for every man is
allowed to rob the man who is next in rank below him.
The poor man who can find no poorer man to rob that he
may pay his due, is the one who suffers most. We saw a
dozen such in the tent at the Basha's camp, chained together,
the neck of each locked in a metal collar; the whole procession was to be marched with the music of that clank-
ing chain to the prison at Tangier, many miles away.

There is no justice in
Morocco. The head-
man of a village
squeezes all he can out
of the nothing that his
people have; the chief
man of the district
levies on the village
headman; the chief
pays tribute to the

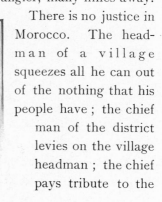

PRISONERS

Governor; the Governor cannot expect to hold his office unless magnificent presents are annually sent to some grand vizier of the court at Fez; and every now and then we hear of the downfall of a grand vizier, who has waxed wealthy, boasted of his possessions, excited the cupidity of his sacred Sultan and paid the penalty, either by suffering the confiscation of his fortune and then exile, or perhaps by drinking, at the command of the all-holy Emperor, a little glass of poisoned tea.

ALCAZAR-EL-KEBIR

We one day tendered in payment for provisions a Spanish dollar somewhat dim and dark. It was refused. "Give me bright shining money," said the man who had supplied us with eggs and milk. "That dark coin looks as if it had been buried; if I attempt to pass it, the chief will send his men to dig around and underneath my house, to see if I have more concealed beneath the floors or in the ground outside."

Next day after our meeting with the Basha, we reach the first interior city of any considerable size, Alcazar-el-Kebir.

"Alcazar the Great," its inhabitants proudly entitle it, and
in its time it has been great. Here there were fitted out, in
the eighth century, the expeditions that went forth to con-
quer Spain and Europe. Later it was taken and held by the
Portuguese until that fatal day in 1578, when, on the battle-
field not far from the city gates, the very flower of the
chivalry of Portugal fell before the fearful onslaught of the
Moorish foe. At Alcazar, Portugal received the death-blow
of her greatness. Before the loss of Alcazar Portugal was
one of the world's great powers. This terrible defeat was the
beginning of the end.

The city is unlike all other cities of the interior, for it was
built by the Portuguese. It is not white, as are the Moorish
cities, but all in dull greys, browns, and soiled and dingy yel-
lows. In the bazaar we purchase more Moorish clothing—
long white garments, far cooler than our riding-suits, and
upon returning in our new attire to the camp, we are greeted
effusively by a dusky gentleman who introduces himself as the
Consular Agent of the United States. Unfortunately his

A THOROUGHFARE

THE SULTAN MULAI EL-HASAN IN TANGIER

kindly words are all
Arabic, of which we do
not understand a word.
Nevertheless Mr. Ham-
man Slawi convinces
us of his good-will by
presenting us with a
pair of yellow slippers,
and manifests his ad-
miration by sitting in
our tent and looking
at us intently for just
two hours and a
half. Long calls

WE PURCHASE MORE
MOORISH CLOTHING

are the custom in Morocco, and when Mr. Slawi finally
departed, he left his son, a fat little chap, to continue
staring at us so that
we might not feel neg-
lected. And when the
boy was finally in-
duced to go, the father
sent the local
s y m p h o n y
orchestra to
serenade u s
in the gloam-
ing, with two
i n s i s t e n t
drums and an
e x a s p e r a t i n g
flute.

We are
compelled to
give these

MR. HAMMAN SLAWI, U. S. CONSULAR AGENT

cacophonic tormentors a present to bring the concert to an end. A present, by the way, is an important element in every Moorish proposition. Presents are the lubricating medium used in the social and political machinery of this ancient empire. Acting upon the advice of former travelers, we have brought with us many gifts for the kaids or sheiks or bashas who show us kindness, or from whom we may

THE SERENADE

desire to obtain favors. A dozen Waterbury watches are reserved for the men who are very great; for lesser nota-bilities we carry other presents, among them, strange to say, all sorts of little toys, like jumping jacks, kaleidoscopes, and automatic animals. These are not intended for the children, but for full-grown men, hoary-headed chieftains who have a passion for such novelties. The Moors are at heart big children, with all the simplicity, deceitfulness, and passion of real children.

And, like unfeeling children, these people are often thoughtlessly cruel. They appear not to notice the wounds caused by the heavy, ill-adjusted harness of the pack mules, or the ugly cut made by the brutal bit in the mouth of Kaid Lharbi's faithful horse. When we remonstrated with our men about this useless cruelty, they answered that the animals are "used to it;" that it is the custom of the country for mules to have raw backs and horses bleeding jaws. The Moslem firmly believes that "whatever is, is right;" and we console ourselves with the assurance of the classic author who asserts that "the souls of usurers are metempsychosed, or translated, into the bodies of asses, and there remain certain years for poor men to take their pennyworth out of their bones."

Later in the day we met with a curious experience. As we began the descent into a broad valley, we saw approaching

TRAVELING THUS EIGHT HOURS EVERY DAY

THE MOUNTAINS OF WAZZAN

us another caravan. When it drew near, we discovered, with pleased surprise, that the man who rode in front was clothed in coat and trousers, evidently a European, a man from our own world, perhaps the only other white-skinned traveler in the land. We shook off the lethargy that results from a long morning in the saddle, and prepared to greet the stranger with smiles and questions, eager to give news of the living world to one who must have been buried for at least many days in this roadless land, eager to send back by him messages to the consul in Tangier. Nearer he comes and nearer, but as yet he makes no sign. Imagine, then, our blank dismay when the caravans pass one another on this narrow trail amid the yellow grain, and the stranger —a German merchant, as we learned afterward—rides past with his Teutonic nose high in air, without a side glance or a nod, without the slightest sign of recognition in answer to our smiles ; for so astonished were we that we could not speak. This exhibition of boorishness, I fear, gave our Moslem followers a sad notion of the love and good-fellowship existing between man and man in the world of unbelievers.

After receiving this cut-direct, we ride on across the grand free landscape, its lines unbroken by trees or houses, where grain grows wild and rots unharvested. In Roman times Morocco was the granary of Europe ; to-day the Moorish authorities prohibit the exportation of all grain. "It is not meet," they say, "that the unbeliever should be nourished by the labor of the faithful."

Thus our days pass until, on the fifth morning of the journey, we halt in a delightful garden on the outskirts of the city of Wazzan. The word "Wazzan" perhaps means nothing to a stranger, but to a Moorish Moslem it is second

"WHERE GRAIN GROWS WILD"

only to Mecca in sacred significance ;
for as Mecca was the home of
Mohammed, the great prophet,
so Wazzan is the home of
the grand Shareef, the most
direct descendant of Mo-
hammed, the most revered
personage in all Morocco.
A connection, however re-
mote, with the prophet's line
is a relationship that insures the
respectful consideration of every
Mohammedan.   To be the most direct
descendant, the grandson-many-times-

DRUDGERY

removed of Fatima, the prophet's daughter and Ali, his
favorite disciple, is to take precedence over Emperors and
Sultans in the sight of every true believer.   And thus the
Shareef of Wazzan, upon whose holy city we now cast our
profane glance, is a greater, holier man than either the

Sultan of Turkey or the Sultan
of Morocco.

   True, these two emperors
trace their ancestry back to the
same sacred source ; but many
true believers call his Turkish

A WELL
IN THE GARDEN NEAR WAZZAN

majesty a renegade and backslider, while the family-tree of
the Moorish Sultan has been so bent and twisted, and its
branches have been so rudely hacked and broken by revolu-
tions, wars, and crimes that a majority of his subjects look
askance upon his pretensions as Commander of the Faithful.
Many of them secretly, some openly, acknowledge the
Shareef of Wazzan not only as the spiritual head of the
Empire,   but also as

THE SACRED CITY OF WAZZAN

its rightful temporal lord.   Fortunately for the internal peace
of the land the Shareefs have been content to exercise imperial
power by suggestion, to receive tithes in lieu of taxes, and to
leave to the Sultan and his ministers at Fez the vexatious
details of the government and the semblance of absolute
authority.   So sacred is this city of Wazzan, so fanatical
are its inhabitants, that we dared not enter its gates until a
military escort sent by the Shareef came to conduct us to the
home assigned us as a residence by that sainted potentate.

It cost our servants several hours' labor to clean the mansion and make it habitable. In the meantime, with Haj as interpreter and Kaid Lharbi to lend dignity to our party, we were escorted by a half-dozen ragged soldiers to the Shareef's palace, which gleams white in the midst of green gardens. There we were received with high-bred dignity and more than ordinary cordiality by the man who, as has been said, is

THE MARKET-PLACE

revered, from Morocco to Madras, as the holiest and greatest representative of Islamism.

We found the Shareef seated on soft cushions beneath a white pavilion in the midst of a luxuriant garden. Around him courtiers were grouped; old men with long, white beards, young men with fierce, hard faces—chiefs of the neighboring tribes. The Shareef, a handsome man, black-bearded and completely robed in simple veils of white, bore his thirty-five years with dignity, despite a suggestion of indolence, almost of lethargy in his manner. Haj approached on hands and knees and kissed the Shareef's garments. We bowed and took the chairs which had been placed for our

comfort just outside the pavilion. The dialogue ensuing
between our host and
g u i d e was deliberate,
cordial, and much em-
broidered with compli-
ments, as is the custom
here in good society. We,
t h r o u g h our spokesman,
thanked his holiness for his
hospitality. He apologizes
for the condition of our
house.

Haj is instructed to ex-
press our complete satisfac-
t i o n . He translates our
crude reply with Moorish
tact a n d delicacy: "My
masters, O Shareef," he
says, "bid me declare that

Photograph by Nelson Ludington Barnes
OUR "PALACE" IN WAZZAN

"THE SHAREEF'S PALACE, WHITE IN THE MIDST OF GREEN GARDENS"

AT HOME IN THE SHAREEF'S CITY

to see thy face is so great joy that they have no thought of minor things; illuminated by the light of thy face, the house becomes a palace, grander than their own palaces in foreign lands." And this sort of thing is actually taken seriously in Morocco! Then, remembering that the presentation of gifts is now in order, Haj continues: "O Shareef, so grateful are my masters for thy kindness that they beg thee to accept a humble present. The youth who wears no beard gladly parts with his precious timepiece, the gift of his father, much prized by him, but still scarcely worthy thine acceptance." Whereupon my friend, with feigned reluctance, detaches from his watch-chain one of our stock of Waterburys, and, as if it had been a gold chronometer, an heirloom in the family, lays it at the feet of Holiness. Holiness graciously accepts the gift, and although he remarks upon the absence of a chain, is apparently well pleased. We are glad that he does not know that we have still nine "Waterbury heirlooms" left in stock.

The interview being over, we return to our residence to find our men indulging in their daily tipple — tea. Kaid Lharbi, sitting aloof as befits his higher rank, brews the tea,

A FORD

and serves it with much ceremony to the rest. Meantime Haj gives us some information regarding the Shareefs of Wazzan. The present saint is, he assures us, a very proper personage, but his late father who owed his title to a clever ruse, was a scandal to the holy name. When his immediate predecessor was upon his deathbed, his ministers implored him to designate which of his many children should succeed him. The old man answered: "In the garden you will find a child playing with my staff. Him shall ye consider the one chosen of God to become Shareef." At this, one of the negresses, a slave, slipped secretly from the room, and finding in the garden the favorite white child of the dying saint, snatched away from the little one the staff, and placed it in the hands of her own little boy, a jet-black imp, who also had the right to call the Shareef father. When the ministers appeared, they bowed low before the negro child, and upon him the mantel of impeccability descended; but whoever has gazed upon him as he appeared in later years will not wonder that the mantle of impeccability was not worn gracefully, and that it frequently slipped off. The charm of European life appealed too strongly to him. He forsook Wazzan, and built for himself a palace in Tangier, where he wined and

Photograph by Nelson Ludington Barnes

THEIR DAILY TIPPLE—"TEA"

dined the foreign diplomats, and ended by falling in love with an English governess. As to his liking for liquor, that sin was forgiven him, since wine cannot enter the mouth of a Shareef — it turns to water at the merest touch of saintly lips. As to his love-affair, that was more serious ; for he married his English sweetheart, to the horror of his people and despite the protests of the woman's friends. The mar-

THE LATE LAMENTED
SHAREEF OF WAZZAN

riage was not performed, however, until he had been forced to sign a contract, abolishing his harem, and making her his wife in a Christian sense. Moreover, one clause provided that should he, "the party of the first part," in spite of all take to himself other wives in the future, a forfeit of

IN CONVERSATION WITH KAID LHARBI

twenty thousand dollars should be paid, per wife, to "the party of the second part." Alas, how many thousands of his great income went to balance this account, so rashly opened with his Christian spouse! After a brief spell of good behavior, the husband fell back into his old ways ; marriages occurred with startling frequency, and, finally worn out by his excesses, the "holiest man in all Morocco," revered by Moslems from the east to the west of Islam, died from the effects of too frequently performing his favorite miracle — that of changing champagne and brandy into water by pouring them between his sacred lips.

The English wife of the wicked old Shareef bore him two sons, now young men. They have been educated abroad, speak English well, and are distinctly up to date. Yet when they travel in Mo- rocco they wear the native dress, and their jour- ney is like a trium- phal pro- gress; all the

people worship them. I have seen large crowds in Tangier fighting only for the opportunity to kiss their gar- ments as they

"BIDS US BEGONE"

rode through the market-place. Neither, however, became grand Shareef on their father's death, for he appointed Sidi Mohammed, his son by a Moorish wife, the man to whom we gave the Waterbury watch. The English widow lives a very secluded life near Oran, in Algeria, but she is loved and revered by the Moors; for while her influence endured, she went about doing good, relieving distress, bringing a little Anglo-Saxon light into the dark lives of her people.

7

And dark indeed must be the lives of the people in the villages near which we pitch our camp. Perhaps a woman would, with great vehemence, bid us begone, lamenting the desolation that will surely come to her village if the strangers camp under the protection of its chief. Her reason is that should we meet with loss from the attack of some wandering band of marauders, this village will be held responsible, and

Photograph by Nelson Ludington Barnes
"YET FLOWERS AND BABIES GROW IN THESE MOORISH VILLAGES"

punishment for offenses committed against us will be visited upon those who, by the sacred laws of hospitality, are bound to protect us.

But disregarding prayers and threats we make ourselves at home ; and finally the women, reconciled, come with their babies to beg for aid and medical advice. Every white man is supposed to possess the power to cure disease, and many were the pitiful appeals made to us for relief and help. We

were asked to treat all kinds of maladies,
but we discovered one unique and hitherto
unknown ailment : ''What is your trouble?''
was asked of a man who came with sadness written on his face. ''Oh!'' he
replied, ''I cannot eat as much as I
should like to.'' Poverty and ignorance
are the common lot, yet flowers and
babies grow in these Moorish villages.

We have now approached a portion of the Beni Hasan territory, a
region inhabited by a tribe whose chief
pursuit is robbery, whose supreme joy is
murder ; and the placing of a guard around

"ON THE LOOKOUT FOR ADVENTURE"

the tent is no longer a mere formality. As yet, however, we
have seen no roving bands ; but next day as we file across
the flower-spotted plain, we observe on the horizon a
number of moving patches of bright color. With lightning-
like rapidity, these flashes of color sweep toward us, each
one resolving itself into a Moorish cavalier, well mounted,
fully armed, and seemingly upon the lookout for adventure. These, then, are Beni Hasan men ! What will they
do to us and how shall we greet them? is our anxious
thought, as they draw nearer, brandishing their rifles, shouting as they ride. The first brief moment of alarm is, however, quickly ended. The chief salutes us cordially ; asks
Haj whence we come, whither we are going ; and then,
desirous of showing honor to us (for foreign travelers are
always looked upon as men of great distinction), he offers to
perform for us a fantasia. The fantasia is an exhibition of
Arabian horsemanship, a sort of glorified cavalry-charge, a
spectacular manœuver, the favorite amusement of the Moorish cavalier, the exercise in which he takes most pleasure and
most pride. It is called by him lab-al-baroud, ''the powder

play.'' A dozen cavaliers, each one a savage, long-haired son of Hasan, advance across the plain, their horses alined, breast with breast. They twirl aloft their richly inlaid guns; then, p u t t i n g their chargers to their fullest speed, the riders rise in the stirrups, seize the reins between their teeth, and sweep toward us in swift majesty. On go the horses at full gallop, still accurately in line. Faster and faster spin the guns above the riders' heads; now muskets are tossed high in air, and descending are caught by strong bronzed hands that never fail. On go the horses; then the men, still standing in the stirrups, their loose garments enveloping them like rapid-flying clouds, at a signal discharge a rousing volley, and under cover of the smoke, check — almost instantaneously with the cruel bits — their panting horses, bloody-mouthed and deeply scarred and wounded by the spurs. This intensely thrilling and picturesque performance is rehearsed before us several times, the chief being proud of his little band of ''rough riders.''

A SON OF HASAN

The men disdainfully examine our English saddles, our horses with docked tails, and laugh at our tiny spurs, for their spurs are sharp spikes three or four inches long. They mockingly challenge us to join them in another fantasia, and to the amazement of the chief my friend accepts the challenge. The long muzzle-loading rifles are charged again, and the entire troop, with an American in its midst, slowly canters away. Facing about, the horsemen form in line and begin to twirl their guns on high. Having no rifle, the stranger draws and flourishes an American revolver. Then, suddenly, the horses leap away, and like a whirlwind the fantasia is upon us. The muskets are discharged; the revolver pops away, and then a mad race begins. Strange to say, the Tangier horse outruns the chargers of the plains, and we see the white helmet of the American flash past, one length in advance of the line of frenzied horsemen!

Chagrined at this defeat, the chief attempts to unseat the victor, charging directly at my friend, who, by a skillful movement, avoids a dangerous collision. Then, spurring after that boasting Beni Hasan tribesman, the American overtakes him, and throws an arm around his neck; and, as they dash on, locked in this embrace, my friend, with a voice that was trained in the Athletic Field at New Haven, shouts a rousing "Rah, Rah, Rah ! — Yale ! " into the ear of the astonished savage, and thus ends our adventure with the wild Beni Hasan band.

A NOONDAY
RESTING-PLACE

Reassured by the amusing outcome of this first encounter, we ride on toward our noonday halting-place. Our marches are so timed that at midday we may find ourselves near some patch of shade. Shade in Morocco is rare indeed, but as every tree and bush between Tangier and Fez is marked on Haj's mental map, we are usually assured of leafy shelter during our noonday rest. Throughout the burning hours from

HAPPY MOMENTS FOR THE MULES

noon till three or four o'clock, we lie at full length amid the flowers, carefully following the shadows as they slowly creep around the trees. The animals, relieved of pack, though not of saddle, browse dreamily, or roll in ecstasy amid the fragant grasses. Our men with Oriental resignation lunch frugally, sit and smoke in silence, or indulge in semi-slumber, with one eye open lest the mules escape. Then, after the sun's rays have lost a little of their torrid sting, we jog on once more in the comparative coolness of the afternoon across the Moorish prairies.

ROUGH RIDERS

Space in Morocco is still a stern reality. The city Fez, to reach which we must travel thus during eleven days, could be reached by rail (were there a railway leading thither) in a half-dozen hours! Apropos of this, let me repeat a scrap of wayside conversation.

"Morocco is indeed a spacious country," said I one day to dignified Kaid Lharbi.

"It is the biggest country in the world," gravely replied the Kaid. Then gently I endeavored to disabuse his mind of this impression by telling of the vastness of the territory of the United States.

"But how long does it take to cross your country?" he inquired.

"We travel five days in fast trains to go from San Francisco to New York," I answered.

"Bah! that is nothing," rejoined our military escort with a sneer of triumph. "To go from Tafilet in the south to Tangier in the north, the fastest caravan must travel *forty days*. You see Morocco is the biggest country in the world!"

Nor can we blame him for his opinion, for the land looks boundless. The grand, free lines of the Moorish landscape are unbroken ; no trees, no houses, no hedges, and no highways are there to spoil the composition of the picture drawn and painted by the master artist, Nature. The country, although fertile, is uncultivated. The horizon seems wider than in other lands. Apparently there is no end, no limit to the landscape. We know that beyond each range of hills there will be revealed a replica of this primeval picture. One scene like this will suc-

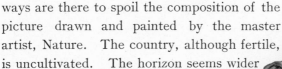

"HAJ"

"SPACE, IN MOROCCO, IS STILL A STERN REALITY"

ceed another with scarce an interruption until the minarets
of Fez shall cut their square majestic outlines against the
southern sky.

Who can describe the floral beauty of these boundless
prairies? — who except Pierre Loti? It was his dainty volume, "Au Maroc," that inspired me with a desire to follow
him into Morocco. When I was reading his beautiful descriptions of the floral mosaic that covers both the plains and
hillsides of the land, I could not easily accept as true the
seemingly exaggerated assertions of the author; his glowing
word-pictures of an " empire carpeted with flowers." Yet he
spoke truly, and as I rode across these broad stretches of
pure white, where marguerites in all their modest loveliness
lie thick upon the greensward, I knew that I had seen it all
before — seen it upon his printed page, as real, as beautifully
vivid as it is to me to-day. To visit Morocco after reading

Pierre Loti is like returning to a land that is familiar, to a land already seen, to a land the charm of which has been revealed in the magic pages of his poetic prose.

For miles and miles this bundle of narrow intersecting trails, the only Imperial Highway of the Sultan of Morocco, leads us on through a veritable garden — between interminable flower-beds. Our foreground is at times pure white, at others purple with a sea of iris flowers, at others scarlet with the blood of anemones, at others yellow with the golden glory of the buttercups and daisies. The mountain slopes and hillsides meanwhile reflect the many colors of the spectrum. It is as if some gorgeous rainbow, shattered in the Moorish heaven, had fallen upon the deserted hills and valleys of this savage, silent land. It is as if the divine Artist had resolved to make this wilderness the palette from which to take the colors for all future landscapes. It is

"THE BIGGEST COUNTRY IN THE WORLD"

as if the sunset of the day before was lingering here to meet
the sunset of the morrow.   It is as if Almighty Allah had
selected the Empire of Moghreb for his sanctuary, and had
spread out upon its sacred floor a prayer-rug of unutterable
beauty, woven by the divine looms — a carpet of heavenly
design to inspire man to fall upon his knees and pray.

This is our life during ten delightful, never-to-be-forgotten
days.   All day we journey southward, pausing at noon "midway 'twixt here and there;" at night we arrive, as my friend
expressed it, at "nowhere in particular," and in the glow of
the sunset we pitch our little camp.   Then, when the evening fire is lighted, the encircling night grows blacker,

AN EMPIRE CARPETED WITH FLOWERS

INTERMINABLE
FLOWER-BEDS

the sur-
rounding
darkness
becomes a
protecting wall,
and we feel almost secure. Our animals are hobbled in a
row before the tent, each with a heap of fresh green grass or
clover. They munch all night; and when we wake, startled
by the cry of a jackal, or by a shout from one of the

"NOWHERE IN PARTICULAR"

"A SEMBLANCE OF A HIGHWAY"

men on guard, we are sure to hear that music of nine
munching mouths.   It is our lullaby, and we fall asleep
again to dream of Fez, the mysterious city which we shall
enter on the morrow.

HAJ BREAKS THE MOSLEM LAW

On the eleventh morning of our journey the semblance of
a highway comes straggling from the south to meet us.   The
countless caravans, crawling toward the holy city, have created this illusion of a road,—a road that will lead us in a few
short hours to the gates of a great city, the fascination of
which, for him who has the slightest love of romance in his
soul, is irresistible.   Fez is no banal, modernized, or tourist-

"MIDWAY 'TWIXT HERE AND THERE"

ridden city, nor is it a mere heap of ugliness and ruin of
which the only charm is a remoteness from the living world.
Fez is a city that has been in its time one of the proudest
and most splendid cities of the Moslem world.   Its fall has
been so gradual that there has been no change, nothing but
a slow decay, so gentle that it has not scarred old Fez, but
beautified it.   Fez, like Venice, requires but a touch of the
imagination, aided by the long shadows of the early morning,

the mystery of twilight, or the silvery magic of the moonlight, to restore it to us as it stood in all its somber beauty eight hundred years ago.

Therefore do we most eagerly await the moment that will reveal to us this crumbling stronghold of a dying race, this beautiful but fragile shell of Moorish civilization,—a civilization that long ago ceased to progress, and, ceasing to progress, has thereby ceased to live.

FEZ

FEZ

THE METROPOLIS OF
THE MOORS

TO modern minds the word "metropolis" suggests a city, great in extent,
in the heart of a thickly populated country;
a place of marvels and of wonderful con-
trivances; a place where commerce has
worn mighty cañons between huge cliffs of masonry; a place
toward which all roads converge; a place whence radiate
interminable rails of steel, along which speed steaming
monsters, annihilating space and bringing vast regions under
the spell of urban supremacy; or else the suggestion is of a
mighty seaport, to which the great ships of the deep bring men
from far-off lands and cargoes from the far ends of the earth.

Metropolis, moreover, means a place where burn the bea-
con-lights of intelligence and culture; where the latest word

THE METROPOLIS OF THE MOORS

of science is spoken; where every day a superstition dies; where seekers after truth come nearest to their goal. A metropolis is the essence of our New Century civilization,— the creation of an irresistible modern impulse, an entity that challenges our admiration and inspires us with awe.

But there is in this world a great city, the metropolis of a nation, which is not like the cities that we know.

APPROACHING FEZ

In the midst of a fertile, smiling wilderness, it is a stranger to all things that are new; its commerce ebbs and flows through channels unknown to the world. At its gates are no railways and no carriage-roads, but it holds infrequent communication with a distant port by means of caravans of mules and camels, and of messengers who run on foot. Its culture is the culture of the Fifteenth Century, its science of still earlier

"IN THE MIDST OF A SMILING WILDERNESS"

date; and truth there is yet hid by clouds of superstition. This city is the essence of the Middle Ages; it is the heart of a nation that was mummified eight hundred years ago by the religion of Mohammed. This city is called Fez; the land of which it is the capital is Morocco.

The first glimpse of Fez is an event in the life of a traveler. Then, if ever, will be experienced one of those delicious little thrills that make their way down the spinal column of a man when he realizes that he has accomplished something of which

he has long been dreaming. And when we, who have long
been dreaming of a visit to the Moor's metropolis, actually
behold it, though it first appears as only a faint line of walls
and towers, almost undiscernible through the rough sea of
heated air-waves that surge between us and the city, now
that Fez at last has risen from this endless plain over which
we have been toiling southward for eleven days, we feel that
we must draw rein, and for a few minutes indulge in the
enjoyment of that creeping thrill. There are so few of them
in life ; the traveler who can remember twenty of these delicious moments in as many years is fortunate above his kind !

Happy in the assurance that a new and thoroughly un-
common experience is opening before us, we ride rapidly on.
Leaving our baggage caravan far in the rear, and halting at
a respectful distance from the walls, we snatch a hasty

"A FAINT LINE OF WALLS AND TOWERS"

Photograph by Nelson Ludington Barnes

" AT ITS GATES, NO RAILWAYS — NO ROADS — "

luncheon before entering the gates of Fez ; and this luncheon
is the last incident of our delightful journey into Morocco. We
have been eleven long days in the saddle. We recall the departure from Tangier, the nights in camp near Berber villages,
the passing glimpse of the city of Alcazar-el-Kebir, and the
visit to Morocco's greatest saint, the Shareef of Wazzan ; nor
can we forget the great sun-flooded land, bright with the colors
of a million-million flowers, across which our little caravan
has struggled at a snail-like pace, crawling scarce twenty
miles between the rising and the setting of the sun.

"THE SUN-FLOODED LAND"

Still with us are the Faithful Five—
the five men who formed our escort.
the men to whom we looked for
comfort, willing service, and protection.   There is Kaid Lharbi,
the military guard, under his
broad-brimmed hat; and as for
the dragoman-in-chief, who can
forget the smiling face of Haj Abd-
er-Rahman?   A marvel of tact and
cleverness was "Haj," but though he
has successfully piloted our fleet of mules

"WHO CAN FORGET THE
SMILING FACE OF HAJ?"

and horses, with their cargoes of tents,
furniture, provisions, cameras, and presents, across trackless
expanses where the only law is the Law of Might, he may well
assume an anxious expression as we approach the gates of
Fez; for there his task will be even more difficult.   Instead
of the lawless, but simple-minded, easily-won people of the
plains, he will now have to deal with city men, men of strong
anti-Christian prejudices, with the proud, ignorant, fanatical,
and cunning population of this untaken
stronghold of Mohammed's faith.   We
shall be met at every turn by a polite
resistance, and although our letters,
obtained in Tangier from the Moorish
Minister of Foreign Affairs, assure us
official protection, we shall be given
to understand that we are not welcome visitors, and that our sojourn
must be made as short as possible.
The surroundings are so smiling
and peaceful that we can scarcely
realize that yonder city is one of the
most fanatical, one of the most rigidly

KAID LHARBI

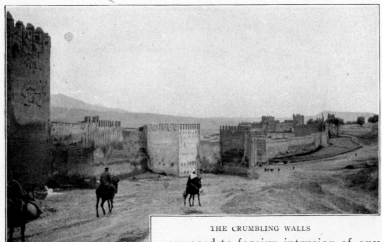

THE CRUMBLING WALLS

opposed to foreign intrusion of any in the world.   Our first impression is that Fez lies on a level plain ; but we find this is not true, for it is spread out on the slopes of an irregular valley. Another view than our first will tell us more of the situation of the place.   I must confess, however, that although my bump of locality is fairly well developed, I found the situation of Fez most difficult clearly to understand, and it was

THE WESTERNMOST STRONGHOLD OF MOHAMMED'S FAITH

only after repeated excursions to the surrounding eminences
that I was able to map out mentally the various quarters of
the town. That there are two great divisions, each almost
independent of the other, we very soon discover.

First, there is the Imperial and official quarter, where
the palaces and gardens of the Sultan and the buildings of
the government are scattered over uncounted acres of high-

" FASS-EL-DJEDID "

walled areas. In native speech, this quarter is called Fass-
el-Djedid ; that is, "Fez, the new," for it is new when measured by the age of Fass-Bali, or Old Fez, which soon reveals
itself to us, lying in a hollow to the left of Fass-el-Djedid.
This is the *medina*, or city proper, wherein are situated the
most sacred mosques, the busiest bazaars, the dwellings of
the poorer classes, and the modest Vice-Consulates of only
two or three European nations. Between the animated
Medina,—a mass of closely packed cubes of white, appearing

when viewed from a distance like a saucer filled with sugar lumps,—and the spacious, stately governmental quarter, lies what is called the garden region.

This portion of the city in part resembles a well-cultivated farming region, open and free of access; in part it is like a labyrinth of narrow high-walled alleys, dividing, with their double barriers of stone and plaster, one mysterious garden from another, isolating the secret retreat of one aristocratic Moor from the perfumed inclosure in which the harem of another is confined. A veritable abode of mystery and beauty is that distant portion of the garden region, a paradise to which the stranger is not welcomed. Nor will the stranger be *persona grata* in any part of Fez if the reports of other travelers are true. Surely, it will be a luxury to be despised by an entire population, and despised because we are that which we are most proud to be, champions of progress, lovers of civilization. And ready to meet the contempt of Allah's

" FASS-BALI "

THE GATE OF NEW FEZ

people, we approach this city.   Near the ruined walls we see
a multitude of whitish forms, now immobile, now swayed as by
emotion. It is an audience composed of men of Fez, gathered
in a sort of natural theater to listen to the dramatic tale of a
famous story-teller.   In ages that are past the white-robed
Greeks came forth from Athens and sat thus in the shadow of
the old Acropolis to listen to the stories of dramatists and poets
whose fame the whole world now knows.   And because of its
suggestion of those ancient gatherings, this assembly takes on
a dignity and an importance in our eyes.   Our coming causes a
diversion ; spectators drop the thread of the speaker's dis-
course, and turn toward us with a scowling curiosity.   There
are no greetings, not a smile, but we are not conscious of any
open rudeness, save that now and then as we ride through the
crowd, we notice that men clear their throats and spit ; this,
however, we expected, for we knew that the presence of a

A MULTITUDE OF SHROUDED FASSIS

THE ARSENAL

Christian so defiles the atmosphere that good Mohammedans
must needs cleanse their mouths
and nostrils after he has passed.

And now one of the great gates of New Fez looms before
us. We enter. For a moment a dampness like that of a
tunnel wraps its cool refreshing blackness about us, and then
we emerge into a spacious age-worn court, which shows us
that the adjective "new" applied to this strange, almost
deserted quarter has only a comparative significance. There
is in the entire city nothing that is really new. And yet this
is not strictly true, for on our right we see a gateway freshly
plastered, freshly painted in pale blue, with piles of cannon
balls upon the top of its pilasters. It is the recently established arsenal of the Sultan. For the Sultan, though averse
to progress and to civilization, has not hesitated to adopt that

9

which is most barbarous in our science,—the modern methods of destruction ; and here he manufactures death-dealing instruments like those invented by the Christians.   We traverse the long, almost de-   serted square, and cross

" FEZ — IN ALL ITS DILAPIDATED REALITY "

the threshold of another gate.   We find ourselves in a tortuous, vaulted corridor, divided into gloomy sections by huge horseshoe arches.   These gates of Fez are surely not designed to facilitate urban circulation, rather are they designed, in case of need, to prevent or at least to impede the rapid gathering of crowds in the great areas around the imperial palace—to isolate the various precincts of the city in case of revolution.

As we pass onward, veiled women observe us with a silent wonder, a few men pause to clear their throats or sneer, a holy beggar crouching in an angle howls after us his incoherent curse. While my horse passes close to one of these ruined pillars, I involuntarily extend my hand and touch the crumbling brick, as if to be assured that all this is not an illusion; that Fez, the city of our dream, does actually exist in all its dilapidated reality; that at last the object of our journey into Morocco has been attained; that our arrival in the Sultan's city is an accomplished fact. Then, followed by our caravan, we pass from under these ponderous arches and enter another court, smaller but not less strange than the first. Here, moving to and fro are a few white-robed beings; but so silently do they stalk along, seemingly unconscious of our presence, that we feel as if we had entered a city of the dead, inhabited only by sheeted ghosts. Already we feel as if the shroud of Islam were being slowly wrapped about us. To the left rise the walls which hide from view the seraglios and palaces of Mulai Al-Hasan III, the Sultan; to the right are

other walls, concealing we know not what mysterious buildings — vast abandoned structures which the stranger never sees.

The Sultans have been reckless builders. We are told that the father of Mulai Al-Hasan began, long years ago, a palace which was designed to be the largest in the world. The walls of one room only were erected, and this room was never even cov-

IN THE GATES

A STOLEN GLIMPSE OF THE IMPERIAL PALACE

ered by a roof.   It forms to-day one of the most extensive public squares of Fez, measuring three hundred by nine hundred
feet.   How the old architects would have solved the problem
of arching this huge empty space, it is impossible to guess.

This is but one of the long series of abandoned squares

"THE EMPTY SPACIOUSNESS OF NEW FEZ"

and public places
across which our es-
cort conducts us,
each separated from
another by crum-
bling walls, pierced
by artistic Moorish
archways. Before
reaching the city
proper, we pass
through a dozen or
more of these arched
portals, so ruinous,
many of them, that
they appear about to
fall and crush us be-
neath tons of cent-

ury-old masonry.   I should but weary you were I to describe our progress in detail ; suffice it to repeat that before
we reach Old Fez we pass through many gates and traverse
interminable, broad, deserted alleys leading between high,
crumbling, battlemented walls, where we are stared at,
muttered at, scowled at, by the shaven-pated youth of Fez,
while more mature citi-
zens exhibit their con-
tempt by striding past
without so much as a

A PUBLIC SQUARE

look.   It argues an immense amount of
self-control to refrain from gazing on such an unusual spectacle as our caravan presented, simply because we were not
true believers.   Nevertheless, there were few among the
better dressed men whom we met, who did not march
severely by, nose in air, eyes front, denying themselves the
satisfaction of an interested stare, because an initial glance
had assured them that we were "unclean Christians."
Though I confess that this reproach, owing to our ten days'
travel overland, and to the scarcity of water in Morocco, was

only too well founded, yet we found it consoling to notice convincing proofs that many of the true believers were also without the virtue that is next to godliness.   Moreover, we intended to reform as soon as we could find a home, while no such admirable intentions can be credited to those who reviled us.

But as for the ladies we encountered — bless their feminine souls! — with them, womanly curiosity proved stronger than religious prejudice.   They frankly halted, turned their pretty faces toward us and gazed up smilingly at the arriving travelers. We must admit, however, that they had the advantage of us ; we were compelled to take for granted both the prettiness and smiles, and it was pleasanter to do so ; moreover, there was nothing else to do.   Still, the features of her who paused on the left, as vaguely molded by the masking haik, were not of

" STARED AT, MUTTERED AT, SCOWLED AT "

Grecian purity. She would have charmed us more had she not drawn her veil so tight. On the right an older woman was more discreet ; like the wise Katisha she believed that it is not alone in the face that beauty is to be sought, so she sparingly dis-played her charms, reveal-ing only a left heel which peo-

"WOMANLY CURIOSITY STRONGER THAN RELIGIOUS PREJUDICE"

ple may have come many miles to see. The fair one in the middle bares her face in most immodest fashion : through an opening at least three quarters of an inch in width two pretty eyes of black are flaming ; and, indeed, it may be set down as an almost invariable rule that the wider the opening 'twixt veil and haik, the prettier the eyes that flash between.

With maledictions on the prevailing style of dress for Moorish beauties, we ride on, passing finally from the empty spaciousness of New Fez into the crowded compactness of the old Medina. Here our pace, always slow, must be made even slower ; our caravan winds at a careful walk into a labyrinth of narrow ways, so dark, so crowded, so redolent of Oriental life, so saturated with the atmosphere of Islam and the East, that we are thrilled with pleasure at the thought that we are for a space to become dwellers in this strange metropolis and to live its life — a life so utterly unrelated to that of the cities whence we come.

" THE CROWDED COMPACTNESS OF THE OLD MEDINA "

First we must secure an abiding-place, for there are no hotels in Fez — at least none in which foreigners could live and remain in possession of their self-respect and sanity. The only places of public entertainment are the Fondaks, where men and mules are lodged and fed. A glance through the door of the Fondak, where our own faithful animals were later in the day entered as boarders for an indefinite period, proved how utterly preposterous it would be for us to depend upon the hotel resources of the capital. Although the packs have been removed, the pack-saddles, each a burden in itself, have not been taken off nor will they be until to-morrow for fear the animals uncovered while heated from exertion might catch cold, fall sick, and die. In fact, the mules have not been free from these cruel weights at any time during the journey of eleven days. Why the idea of suicide does not appeal to the Morocco mule is but another of the unaccountable problems of the land.

Convinced that hotel-life in Fez has no attraction for us, we follow Haj toward the palace of the Governor, where, thanks to our official letters, we expect to find that ample provisions for our comfort have been made. We halt at last before an unpromising door, in a deep and narrow street. The palace of the Basha is not extremely imposing in its exterior, but we know that in Morocco bare outer walls often hide undreamed-of splendor, and that dirty, dingy streets may surround pavilions and gardens of unsuspected beauty. Therefore it is with confidence that we in-

"A LABYRINTH OF NARROW WAYS"

trust our letters, long, beautifully written documents in Arabic, to the attendant at the door. He disappears; we wait; he remains out of sight; we continue to wait.

For three long, mortal hours this

THE BEST "HOTEL" IN FEZ

endures. Evidently the Basha is deliberating deeply upon the proper disposition of his unwelcome visitors. Now and then an official comes out to look us over, but nothing is done. Soldiers and servants are sent away on errands, and seem never to return. We sit, meanwhile, mute protests at the door. Knowing our helplessness, we curb our anger and impatience, and endeavor to conceal our weariness from the scornful citizens who pass with haughty sneers, happy to see two Christians awaiting the Basha's pleasure.

At last a servant comes with a reply. On receiving it, Haj flies into a passion, and orders the caravan to follow him, and away we file through the crowded streets, Haj gesticulating wildly and shouting loud enough for all to hear that the Basha has attempted to extort money from the foreign visitors, who are great lords, whereas he is bound by instructions from the Minister at Tangier to lodge them at the expense of the city. And this is true; it is the policy of the government to provide gratis a house for foreign visi-

AT THE BASHA'S DOOR

From a unique photograph by an anonymous Algerian pilgrim   MECCA, THE HEART OF ISLAM

tors to Fez. This policy is prompted not by a generous
spirit of hospitality, but by a desire to control the movements of the strangers. It is feared that if the foreigner is
permitted to pay rental for his house, he may in some way
establish a vague right to occupy it longer than is consistent with the desires of the government. This might
prove awkward and lead to complications. It is much
simpler to make the foreigner a guest, who cannot refuse
to move on when politely notified that his abode is needed
for another visitor.

In our case, however, the Basha has demanded payment
for the house, and Haj, knowing well how to deal with this
emergency, is leading us with ostentatious indignation toward
the city gates, breathing as he rides loud threats that he will
report our treatment to our friend, the Moorish Minister of
Foreign Affairs, and declaring that we will, meantime, pitch
our camp outside the walls, and hold the Governor responsible for any injury suffered at the hands of prowling robbers.
His shrewd tactics prove ef-
fectual ; for as we are passing

MYSTERY-PERVADED STREETS

THE SUNNY ALLEYS OF THE GARDEN REGION

through one of the pretty alleys of the Garden Region, we are overtaken by servants of the Governor. Repentant, he has sent them with the keys of a villa that he has assigned to us. We follow the Governor's retainers toward the heart of the aristocratic quarter, through a perplexing labyrinth of sun-flooded alleys, where the redundant vegetation of the silent, surrounding gardens overflows the sky-line, or bursts through cracks in the old masonry. We know not whither we are being led; we scarcely dare hope that we shall be permitted to abide in this delightful residential region, and we fear that some abandoned house will be made to serve us as a semi-prison. And soon it seems that our worst fears are to be realized, for although the caravan is halted in the garden region, it is in the dingiest and narrowest of its streets, before the lowest and the darkest of its doors.

When Pierre Loti came to Fez and saw for the first time the entrance to his house, he immediately exclaimed: "But this is not a human habitation! One might be pardoned for thinking it the entrance to a rabbit hutch; and even then they must be very poor rabbits to live in such a place."

The door of our promised abode looks like the outlet of a sewer or the entrance to a pig-sty. And Haj, who has buoyed up our hopes with descriptions of t h e palace we were soon to occupy in Fez, receives reproachful glances. We fear h i s "palaces" no more deserve their name than did his "forests" and his "lakes" and "rivers," for to him a clump of half a dozen trees was a "*forêt magnifique!*"

"IN THE NARROWEST AND DINGIEST STREET"

a muddy pool "*un lac superbe,*" and a slimy streamlet, "*une rivière claire et belle.*" And now his "*palais splendide*" bids fair to be — a dirty prison.

But the arrival of o u r pack-mules leaves us no

"THE LOWEST, DARKEST DOOR"

time for reproaches or complaints.   The caravan completely
blocks the circulation of the neighborhood.   The pack-mules,
too broadly loaded, get stuck fast in the narrow street, and
we are compelled to back them out and discharge the cargoes
at a neighboring street-intersection.   Our folding beds and
chairs, our gaily-colored rugs and cushions, our kitchen outfit, and our   photographic kit
are heaped   up in the public

BETWEEN SILENT GARDENS

thoroughfare, pending the disappearance of the
animals.   But happily, owing to the blockade, there are no
passers-by ; else the major portion of our goods might also
disappear.   A sound of rushing water fills the air, for one of
the rapid canals that irrigate the gardens and turn the flour-
mills of Fez, here flows beneath the street.   It makes a music
very grateful to the ears of those who are new come from the
torrid prairies of the provinces.   Truly, it will be pleasant to
rest for a few days and listen to that music, no matter how

distasteful our abode may prove to be. Let us, then, with
resignation crawl through our dingy door and make ourselves
at home.

Accordingly, we stoopingly grope through a low dark
passage, then—stand erect and gasp with pleasure! Aladdin,
when for the first time he rubbed the magic lamp, could not
have been more thoroughly delighted or surprised. Before

" DISCHARGING CARGO "

us is a dainty villa, snowy white ; around it a delicious garden,
more than an acre in extent. The fact that everything is
purely Moorish, that no hint of European occupation can be
seen, and the conviction that our home differs in no important
detail from the dwellings of our aristocratic neighbors, gives
added charm to our abode, added delight to the thought of
sojourn here in this exotic atmosphere. It is resolved that
we shall occupy the upper story, that our men shall find
lodgings in the lower rooms, while for the noonday nap, the
10

PACK-MULES STUCK FAST BETWEEN THE WALLS

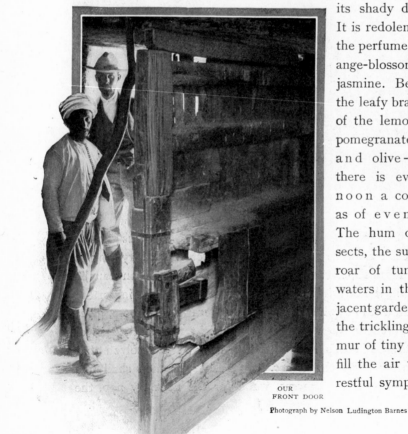

OUR
FRONT DOOR

Photograph by Nelson Ludington Barnes

promenade, or a quiet hour with a book, our pretty garden offers us its shady depths. It is redolent with the perfume of orange-blossoms and jasmine. Beneath the leafy branches of the lemon and pomegranate, fig- and olive-trees, there is even at noon a coolness as of evening. The hum of insects, the subdued roar of tumbling waters in the adjacent garden, and the trickling murmur of tiny canals fill the air with a restful symphony.

OUR VILLA

OUR MOORISH GARDEN

We have forgotten the rudeness of our welcome; we have shut out the grim, hostile city; we are at last at home in Fez. We are as safe as if shut up in jail. In fact, like all foreign visitors, we, too, must record among our sensations that of being prisoners while within the walls of Fez; but we are very willing prisoners, and when the hour of dinner is

Photograph by Nelson Ludington Barnes   AT HOME IN FEZ

announced, we cheerfully climb the tiny spiral stairway to our roomy cell, and with this first meal begin the routine of our daily home life in the Sultan's city.

We have simply pitched camp in the great upper chamber of the house, spread out the rugs, set up the beds, the chairs, and tables, and made ourselves as comfortable as possible. The windows are merely huge openings in the wall, unglazed, with metal bars and heavy wooden shutters. The floor is neatly tiled, the walls are whitewashed, and the ceiling is of

Photograph by Nelson Ludington Barnes

WILLING PRISONERS

wood. Our
five attendants
have taken
possession of
the lower
floor. There
also Haj has
installed his
little cuisine,
and is
indus-
triously
encour-
aging
a tiny

HAJ'S CUISINE

charcoal fire with a fan. Sitting near, intently observing his
culinary operations, is a young Jewish woman, who brought
a recommendation from the British Vice-Consul, and was
engaged to act as maid-of-all-work, to help five helpless men

to bring order and com-
fort out of the chaos that
reigns here on the day
of our arrival. That she
does not lack for occupa-
tion is proved by the as-
pect presented by our
courtyard dur-
ing the painful
period of in-
stallation in
our exquis-
ite Moorish
home. Pack-
baskets, bed-

THE JEWISH MAID-OF-ALL-WORK

ding, blankets, furniture, and dishes had been dumped there in confusion ; but through the efforts of our Hebrew house-keeper, all things are quickly put to rights, the court resumes its wonted air of Oriental languor, the little fountain sings on its uninterrupted song, and the atmosphere of romance once more envelopes house and court and garden. To fill our cup of happiness, a messenger arrived, bringing a bulky

CHAOS IN THE COURTYARD

packet of letters from America ; for a courier of the British consul, who left Tangier one week after our departure, has arrived in Fez the day of our arrival, having run on foot the entire way, one hundred and seventy miles in four days' time ; while we, encumbered with a baggage caravan, have been eleven days upon the way.

We remain a day and night in our new abode before venturing out into the streets. We shall now cautiously commence a series of expeditions — one cannot call them strolls or promenades — across and round about the town. The objective-point of our first expedition is the office of our banker. We descend from the high-lying Garden Region, and enter the ruinous streets of the Medina. We are accompanied by Haj, for without a guide we should soon go astray. We are followed by Kaid Lharbi, our military escort, it being most imprudent for the foreigner to walk abroad unaccompanied by a guard. To photograph in the streets of Fez is difficult

STREETS LIKE VAULTED TUNNELS

to the verge of impossibility. First, there is the Mohammedan prejudice against picture-making, the reproduction of the likeness of living things being prohibited by the Koran, which says: "Every painter is in hell-fire, and Allah will appoint a person at the day of resurrection for every picture he shall have drawn, to punish him; and they will punish him in hell. Then, if you must have pictures, make them of trees and things without souls." Had the photographer existed in Mohammed's day, he would undoubtedly have had a special verse in Scripture devoted to his case; as it is, the faithful call the camera a "painting-machine," and class its

TRELLISED THOROUGHFARES

manipulator with the impious artists whose instruments of crime are brushes. Even though this difficulty may be overcome by cunning, the very streets and structures conspire with the people to foil the eager camerist. Many of these streets are vaulted tunnels, illuminated only here and there by bands of light; others are roofed by vine-covered trellises, that give them the appearance of interminable arbors, through which faint squares of light flitter and fall upon the unpaved ground; still others are so narrow and are cut between such tall dark walls, that never by any chance do rays of sunshine illuminate their depths. Street life in Fez is vividly suggestive of subterranean existence. There is a dark-cellar-like cool-

"AMONG RESUSCITATED
MEN IN THEIR SHROUDS"

ness, which, combined with the ghostly stride and costume of
the inhabitants, gives us the impression of being in the cata-
combs among resuscitated men in their shrouds. Ghostly indeed is the dress of the rich old men in Fez,—a dress that
gives its wearers the dignity of Roman senators. What a superb figure for the ghost of Hamlet's father one well-remem-
bered old gentleman would make! He is, however, Haj's
uncle, and greets our guide, his nephew, very cordially. Haj,
rascal that he is, knowing that we care more for snap-shots
than for introductions, always arranges when he meets a friend
or relative to detain him in conversation, in the best illuminated portion of the street, thus giving us invaluable opportunities for secret portraiture. Then, after he has heard the

"click!" that
comes from what
appears to be an
innocent brown
paper parcel under
my right arm, Haj,
with many com-
plimentary phras-
es, presents us to
our visitor, intro-
ducing us as men of
great distinction
from America.

Presently we
emerge from the
dim bazaars, and
find ourselves in a
small, deep, pub-
lic square. On
one side is a semi-
ruinous water

AN EXCHANGE

fountain, roofed with tiles
and decorated with mosaics.
Before us is a stately portal,
the entrance to a commer-
cial exchange, a headquart-
ers for the better class of
merchants. It dates from
the time when Fez was the
commercial center of a rich
and very prosperous empire,
when the merchandise of the
world found here a profitable
market. The building now
is sadly out of repair, like
almost every other building

HAJ GREETS A GENTLEMAN OF FEZ

in the city. To make repairs in Fez is sacrilegious. If a

"REPAIRS ARE SELDOM MADE IN FEZ"

structure crumbles
and decays, the
owner with resigna-
tion folds his hands
and murmurs, "It
is the will of Allah ;
it is written," and
forthwith, grateful
for this mark of di-
vine favor, hies him
to the mosque and
prays.

The Mohamme-
dan strictly fulfils
his religious observ-
ances. During the
hour of prayer the
quarter is deserted ;

TRADERS "ON THE CURB"

an hour later business is resumed, and the wheels of metro-
politan commerce, released for a short space from the religious
brake, again revolve with many a squeak and crunch, clogged
as they are by superstition and neglect.   Yet for the artist or
lover of the picturesque, it would be difficult to find a more
attractive crowd of business men.   And these Moorish archways, fountains, tiled roofs, and age-eaten arabesques are
still most beautiful, even in dilapidation more beautiful,

THE OFFICE OF THE AMERICAN CONSULAR AGENT

perhaps, than when in all their freshness they were the pride
and admiration of generations of Fassis, long since gathered
into Paradise.   We are informed that our banker, who is
also the consular agent for the United States, has offices
within a certain medieval business block ; and as we are in
need of funds, and also desirous of meeting our representative, we push through the trading throng and enter the patio,
a spacious inner court four stories deep.   Four tiers of
galleries rise about us, all richly finished in old woodwork,

elaborately carved, but sharing in the slow decay of the entire
building.   Our consular agent, whose office door stands open
on the left, is (as we have been told) a native Jew, by name,
Benlezrah ; by occupation, a merchant, broker, and money
lender ; and by nationality, thanks to the " protection "
system prevalent in Morocco, an American citizen.   Benlezrah admits that his consular duties are not engrossing, nor
are they profitable ; for he receives no pay except in the form
of infrequent fees ; but he holds to his office most tenaciously
because the United States has power to naturalize all its
servants in Morocco, and to grant them what are called
" protection papers. "   Were he not thus protected by some
foreign power, the Sultan's assessor would, he assures us,
soon strip him of his comfortable fortune gained in commerce.   A few days later we visited Mr. Benlezrah at his
home in the Jewish quarter, where we find him surrounded
by his family.   A high sepulchral bed, something between an
Oriental shrine and the proscenium of a Punch and Judy
theater, is the dominating feature of his drawing-room.
During our call our host tells us more about the protection

JUST DIRT

system. It appears that all rich men in Morocco are subject to the most barefaced robbery by the Sultan and his ministers. When in need of funds, the government notifies its chosen victim that a large contribution for the coffers of the sacred Sultan will assure the giver of the imperial favor, and that a refusal to obey the hint will be followed by imprisonment or

MR. BENLEZRAH AT HOME

confiscation, or both. But men protected by foreign powers cannot be imprisoned or punished until tried for their offenses before the consular court in Tangier, and are therefore practically insured against the cupidity of corrupt imperial officials. Thus every Moor or Jew, possessed of wealth,

11

ENIGMAS

TWO OF THE SULTAN'S CABINET

desires the protection of a foreign nation. Protection being such a boon, abuses have naturally attached themselves to the granting of it.

The Moorish government has complained that consuls of the European nations, yes, even of the United States, have been guilty of selling for cash the protection of their respective flags to wealthy Moors and Jews. To the Jew, protection is indeed a special blessing, since it gives him the right to ride on horseback or muleback through these streets, where other Jews must walk. It permits him to pass the doorways of the mosques without stopping to remove his shoes, while other Jews must bare their feet each time they near the sacred gates.

It must be remembered that the current calendar in Fez is not that of A. D. 1907; but it is for the year 1325,* after the Hegira of Mohammed, and the Moors are about six centuries behind the times!

These Mohammedans of Fez not only do not permit the Jew to pass the mosque with shoes upon his feet, but they do not permit any infidel to enter their sacred places; they do not permit Jew or Christian to pause to look in at the doors, and there is one mosque, the Shrine of Mulai Idrees, the founder of Fez, so holy that no unbeliever is permitted even to approach it. Across the streets leading thither barriers are placed; the Moors stoop and pass under them; the Christian

* The Mohammedan lunar year being several days shorter than our solar year, makes the Moslem New Year's Day a movable feast, which in the course of centuries works its way through all the seasons. The year 1325, after the Hejira of Mohammed, began on February 14th, Anno Domini, 1907.

THE FUEL MARKET

and the Jew, on pain of
death, must go no farther.
Then across other streets
bars are placed to mark the
point beyond which men are
not allowed to pass at certain hours.

One portion of the cool
cellar-like bazaar is sacred
to the women, who, tem-
porarily embarrassed, bring
hither objects that they wish
to sell. Apparently they are
not eager to attract pur-
chasers, for they hide whatever they may have beneath
their haiks ; but now and
then a man approaches, and
an embroidered vest, a piece
of silk, a jewel or a ring is
reluctantly brought forth and
passed across the barrier in

NEARING A PORTAL OF THE KARŪEEÏN

exchange for silver coins ; then one white, shrouded figure
rises and fades away amid the ghostly throng. To us, new-
comers to this land of mystery, it is as disconcerting to face
a crowd of these women, as for the soldier to stand unmoved
before masked batteries. We are conscious that two score
of bright, black eyes are leveled at us, but we cannot read
the message they project — the faces that would make the
message legible are veiled. Are the lips curled in scorn of
the infidel ? Are smiles of ridicule excited by his strange
foreign dress, so pitifully convenient and unpicturesque, so
tight, so graceless, when compared to the splendid sweep of
the Moorish costume ? Or, in some faces, is there written a

deep, bitter yearning for knowledge of the outside living world,— the world of to-day, of which we stray moderns come here as reminders? But as we wander ever through the bazaars, meeting everywhere the same impassive, un-curious expressions on the uncovered faces of the men, we are inclined to believe that to the Moor, Morocco is the world,— that for him, outside its borders, geographically or intellectually, there is nothing worthy his consideration. A few progressive Moors, so we were told, evince a shadowy interest in the universe at large by subscribing for a daily paper. This paper is not printed in Fez, where journalism is unknown, it comes from far-off Cairo on the Nile, and reaches its eager Moorish readers after a voyage of seven days by sea and eight by land.

Remembering these things, it is difficult to believe that Fez is, in the eyes of the Mohammedans, an important seat of learning, but so it is ; for does not the famous university and mosque, known as the Karûeeïn stand in the very heart of Fez? The Karûeeïn, a sort of inner "holy city" is, next

to the mosque of Mulai Idrees, the most sacred inclos-ure in Fez : As we approach it, we are warned by Haj that Christians are not permitted even to pause and glance into its courts when passing any of its many portals. The imperfect pictures that will reveal to you vague glimpses

A COURTYARD OF THE INVIOLABLE KARÛEEÏN

of its dark corridors
and sunlit patios are
the result of oft-re-
peated efforts, risks,
and subterfuges.
The entrances are
jealously guarded by
the faithful ; the Jew
or Christian who
lingers on the thresh-
old is rudely jostled
by t h e passers-by,
and if he does not
take the hint, a sud-
den surging of the
crowd sweeps h i m
away. Three morn-
ings w e r e devoted
to vain attempts to
bring the camera to
b e a r upon t h o s e
gates. But finally a

A KIOSK OF THE KARÛEEÏN

fourth attempt, aided by strategy, met with success. Opposite
every gate are groups of beggars, crouching in the narrow
street. Strolling with ostentatious carelessness, the camera,
wrapped like a paper parcel, under my arm, I pause before
the beggars, my back turned to the sacred entrances, and
fumble in my pocket for stray coppers. No one sees any
reason for interfering with the charitable stranger ; but,
mingled with the chink of the coins dropped into the outstretched palms, there might have been heard the clicks of a
photographic shutter, fired almost at random, and these
pictures here shown are the rewards of my charity, so hypo-
critically bestowed. I had had faith in my ability finally to

accomplish my sinful task ; I had been buoyed up by the hope of success, but while I had not charity, my efforts did not profit me.

The Karûeeïn is the greatest educational institution of western Barbary. Nor must we smile to hear it called by so proud a name. Its past entitles it to the respect of the world. It ranked with the great colleges of Moorish Spain — with Cordova itself — as a seat of learning, and hither came not only Moslems, from all corners of Islam, but also noble gentlemen from England, France, and Spain, to complete their educations. Yes, as we glance into another patio, where a green tiled kiosk recalls the Court of the Lions of the

Alhambra, we must not forget that here philosophy once flourished, here astronomy, mathematics, and medicine once were more fully developed than at any other place in the contemporary world. In the inaccessible library of the Karûeeïn, the lost books of Euclid are said to be moldering, also many classics, fragments for which scholars have been seeking. But these things will not be brought to light

WHERE MEN ARE TAUGHT BY "INTELLECTUAL MUMMIES"   until the death-knell

of Morocco's independence shall have sounded.   The Karûeeïn
to-day stands here in the heart of Fez, as the center of resistance to all progress, as the embodiment of slumber ; yet
here are gathered even in our day more than a thousand
students, four hundred of them supported by an endowment
fund dating from the twelfth century.   That is, their food is

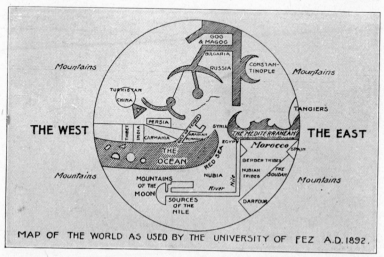

MAP OF THE WORLD AS USED BY THE UNIVERSITY OF FEZ A.D. 1892.

provided for them gratis, their lodging costs them nothing,
for they sleep under the arcades of the Mosque or in its
spacious courts. They are taught by wise men —"Taleebs"—
men who are intellectual mummies. They learn to repeat
the Koran word for word ; they learn to hate the unbeliever,
to scorn his science and inventions, to turn their backs upon
all things that are new ; they are encouraged to cling to the
old dream of Islam, and to worship the God of their fathers
in this holy mosque. They are taught the forms and simple
ceremonials of the Moslem faith ; to wash the feet at the
fountain before entering the sanctuary ; to leave their yellow,
heel-less slippers in the court ; to kneel, or rise, or prostrate
themselves at proper intervals ; to pray five times each day ;
to turn their faces while they pray toward the sacred city

Mecca in the East ; to drink no wine, to eat no pork, to keep
with cruel rigor the long fast of the Ramadan, when for forty
days they may not touch food, drink, or tobacco between the
rising of the sun and the going down of the same. As for
their secular teaching, it is refreshingly original.   A map of the
world, the use of which is sanctioned by the faculty,
throws much interesting light
upon the Moorish geographic
point of view.   An
examination of the

" AIR OF DESOLATION "

map shows that Tangier,
although a Moorish port, is placed on
the north side of the Mediterranean, while Spain, apparently,
is next door to Morocco, on the coast of Africa.   The results
of Stanley's explorations are outlined with remarkable angu-
larity and distinctness around the sources of the Nile and the
Mountains of the Moon.   England, though not named, is
represented by one of the islands just north of India and
Thibet ; moreover, the latest Moorish expedition to the north
pole has evidently reported that Gog and Magog abide amid
the frozen seas, for they figure on the map.

"FIRST COMES A SQUAD OF SOLDIERS"

Every spring the students
of the Karûeeïn, who are called "Tholbas," go forth from
Fez, and pitch a great camp in the plain. They elect one
of their number "Sultan of the Tholbas," and to him all
must pay reverence. Even the veritable Sultan himself
must ride out in state and call upon Student Sultan in the

THE THOLBA CAMP

MODERN MOORISH SOLDIERY

Tholbas' camp, treating him as an Imperial brother.

The expenses of this scholastic picnic are paid by contributions exacted by the Tholbas from the citizens of Fez.

Returning from our visit to this camp, we make our way
once more into the official quarter of New Fez, through which
we passed so hurriedly the day of our arrival.   The same grim
walls are there, the frowning towers, and the air of desolation.
To our great regret we have learned that the Imperial Master,
Mulai El-Hasan, Sultan of Morocco, will not return to Fez
until long after our departure.   He is at present on the march
across the southern deserts, returning from a journey of eigh-
teen months' duration to the rebellious province of Tafilet,
on the border of the Great Sahara.   Small wonder that the
New Fez appears deserted; for when his Imperial Majesty
goes upon a journey, he is followed by no less than a quarter

of the population of Fez, 30,000 people, — officials, soldiers, servants, and wives and slaves. But we are, nevertheless, to see a remnant of his retinue, for suddenly a crowd appears as if by magic, and the square takes on an air of life and animation.

First comes a squad of soldiers, marching to the beating of a drum. They wear the hideous modern uniform of the new Moorish army — an army that has been created within the past few years by a foreign officer on the Imperial staff, a Scotchman, Kaid Maclean, who has transformed the ragged unkempt hordes of his Imperial Master into an army with some pretensions to discipline and equipment, although to us it

THE GATHERING AT THE GATE OF JUSTICE

WITH THE BRITISH VICE-CONSUL

appears almost grotesque. The uniform chosen gives the private soldier the aspect of a simian pet of an organ-grinder, a little overgrown. Judging by their appearance we are prepared to see these warriors doff their caps and pass them around for coppers ; but this is less the fault of the soldiers than of the military tailor ; the same men robed in long flowing garments would, in all probability, appear as dignified as the civilians. We had the curiosity to examine their weapons, and we were rewarded by discover-

CAPTURING A FORT WITH CAMERAS

Photograph by Nelson Ludington Barnes

ing several muzzle-loading rifles, bearing the inscription, "Springfield, Massachusetts, 1865."

The first awkward squad is followed by another and another, until the great square, bisected by a long procession of those red-coated fighters, appears like a ravine through which there flows a river of blood. Meantime, from the portal of the palace there emerges with solemnity and slowness a stately company of white-robed Moors, some mounted upon superbly harnessed mules, followed by spotlessly arrayed dignitaries and courtiers on foot; and in the midst of these rides the Viceroy of Fez. We dared not raise our cameras as he passed, for the crowds regarded us with hostility, and the picture we secured shows only his retreating form, towering above the heads of his attendants.

"THERE ARE GARDENS AND ORCHARDS"

A DIPLOMATIC OUTING

The procession enters the huge "Gate of Justice." On the left we discern a line of crouching figures, those who have come to make or answer charges before the autocratic tribunal. There is no appeal from the instantaneous decisions given by the old Vizier of Justice. Happy the citizen who, thanks to the protection afforded him by a foreign consul, is exempt from being dragged to this bar of so-called justice!

"TRAILS THAT ARE ALMOST ROADS"

The only Anglo-
Saxon representative
in Fez is His Bri-
tannic Majesty's
Vice-Consul, Mr.
Mac Iver Mac Leod.
For downright per-
tinacity commend
me to this man, who,
in the face of an en-
tire nation's opposi-
tion, planted himself
in Fez, established a
vice-consulate, and
stuck to his post un-
til the Moors gave up
the fight and resolved
to tolerate his per-
manent presence in

THE VICE-CONSULAR VILLA

their holy city. With Mr. Mac Leod we enjoy frequent excursions roundabout the city, to the nearer mountain crests,
and to the abandoned forts upon the hill-tops, whence
splendid views of Fez are to be had. One day, finding no
practicable doorway to one of those deserted strongholds, we
entered boldly through the embrasure where years ago the
noses of old cannon had breathed threatenings above the
once-rebellious city. Affrighted at our daring, my youthful
camera-bearer dropped the case and fled.

There are orchards and gardens in the environs of Fez,
and there are trails that are almost roads, radiating in all
directions. We are invariably accompanied by an escort
when we ride forth from Fez ; the country roundabout is not
safe. The British Vice-Consul always brings his followers,
and insists that we shall order out Kaid Lharbi, our pictur-

12

BRITISH SOCIETY IN FEZ

esque old soldier-chaperon, every time we venture beyond the crumbling walls.

The Vice-Consulate is in the old Medina, in the heart of Fez; but Mr. Mac Leod lives in the garden region. A pretty Moorish villa has been transformed into an English home, presided over by the Vice-Consul's mother, who has exiled herself from England to spend her days with her courageous son in Fez.

"But I am not the only Christian woman in Fez," Mrs. Mac Leod assures us, in reply to our remark that she must sorely miss the companionship of people of her own race and religion. "If you will dine with us on Sunday, you will meet the five Tabeebas." We accepted the invitation, and met the "five Tabeebas," each one a study for a statue of Lot's wife after she had so unwisely looked over her left shoulder. Pillars of salt they look, and in truth they are the salt of this cruel Moorish land. They are Christian women, angels of mercy, missionaries,—but not ordinary missionaries,—theirs is a *medical* mission,—a mission through which no energy is wasted, against which no criticism can be urged.

Among them are three English women, one Irishwoman, and one Scotch lassie. Their work is, of necessity, chiefly with the bodies rather than with the souls of those they seek to aid; for they realize, as every sane-minded Christian must, that to Christianize Moorish Mohammedans is an impossibility unless the missionary first wins the confidence and love of the people through many palpable and self-evident deeds of benevolence.

The dress of these women is but another expression of their innate tact. If they insisted upon going abroad in the streets with uncovered faces, they would immediately lose the respect and confidence of the people who have learned to love them for their numberless good works. They occupy a large house in the densely populated quarter, a home which is by turns a school or a hospital. Here they teach Moorish girls many useful things; here every day they receive and treat,

THE TABEEBAS

THE TABEEBAS TEACHING

free of charge, as many patients as present themselves. One afternoon while we were taking tea with the Tabeebas, they were repeatedly called from the room to dress a wound, apply an ointment, or give advice to some poor sufferer. Of course we were not permitted to see the Moorish girls who come to the Tabeebas' school. To secure a photograph of them my camera was lent to one of the Tabeebas, who secretly made an exposure from behind a door that stood ajar. Did the parents of these young girls know of the making of the picture, there would be no pupils here upon the morrow. The faces in the group are faces on which no man may look, unless he be the father, brother, or husband.

Let us steal away through the mysterious, fascinating streets and byways that lead us, with a hundred puzzling turns, back to our peaceful villa.

It is needless to say that our neighbors have not called upon us, nor indicated by any sign that they are conscious of

our presence in this aristocratic precinct.   Walls from fifteen
to twenty feet in height surround our garden, cutting us off
completely from the public streets and from the garden of our
next-door neighbors.   Our curiosity concerning that adjoin-
ing garden and the family that dwelt therein increased from
day to day.   Apparently an interminable picnic is in progress
there ; for three days past we have been hearing the shouts of
children at play and the strange shrill cry peculiar to Moorish
women, a piercing tremolo, to which they give utterance in
token of joyfulness.   It might be called the "college yell" of
these Oriental wives—pupils in the school of submission.

Finally we can resist no longer ; we must learn what is
passing there on the other side of that high wall.   But how?

OUR VILLA FROM THE STREET

A STOLEN PEEP OVER GARDEN WALL

We dare not show our heads for fear some jealous Moor may smash them. We resolve to make a cat's-paw of the faithful camera to snatch curiosity-satisfying chestnuts out of the fire of Moslem exclusiveness. We climb a ladder, lift the camera, upside-down, above the wall, take aim by looking up into the inverted finder, fire, and withdraw precipitately. The result was worth the risk and effort. The plate revealed a scene from private family life in Fez,—the picture of a rich Moor's wives and children attended by black slaves, taking their ease in the absolute seclusion of their garden, brewing and drinking Moorish tea, as they sit on a tiled platform that surrounds a bathing tank. The foreshortening of the figures may be at first a trifle puzzling; remember we are looking, or, rather, the camera is looking down upon the group from over a garden-wall that is not less than twenty feet in height.

Fortunately, the attention of the family had been attracted by something occurring just out of our range of vision, though

DISCOVERED!

we knew nothing of this at the time. The negative was not developed till we reached America, so the camera recorded a scene which we ourselves have never looked upon. Encouraged by the silence following our first attempt, we chose another section of the wall and repeated our manœuver. Unfortunately a preliminary click was heard by our sitters, whose startled expressions, faithfully registered, prove that they have seen the guilty lens and shutter winking at them from the summit of the wall. Some have already hid their faces, others are apparently crying out in protest ; even the dog, like a good Mohammedan, turns his back to the "painting machine." The unique picture tells us what manner of women is concealed by the shroudlike garments, which are worn in the streets and which make women, be they young, old, rich, poor, beautiful, or ugly, appear as like, one to another, as are bales of woolen cloth. Street life in Fez is for women a perpetual masquerade, a lifelong domino party. But in these high-walled gardens all the participants unmask, throw off their haiks, and during the home hours regain an individuality of visage, form, and dress. This revelation of the inner life of Fez makes the city seem more human to us, less like a city of spectaters, ghosts, and animated mummies. Nevertheless these people seem not quite real to us, for we did not actually see them, nor did they see us, face to face. Next day two huge black men-slaves came to notify us that if any more mysterious boxes appeared over the garden-wall their master, now absent, should be informed, and our departure hastened.

"GREETS US WITH LOUD HOWLS"

Photograph by Nelson Ludington Barnes

NEIGHBORS

We had one neighbor, however, who was more sociable; in fact, he became painfully familiar. He lived at a street corner where he enjoyed a squatter-right, for he had been squatting there without intermission for five years or more. The man is crazy. He invariably greets us with loud howls, and insists upon it that we are "his mothers!" Then, like a whining child, he teases for matches with which to light a fire. He has a mania for collecting brushwood, building fires, and then extinguishing them by calmly sitting down upon the flames, much to the detriment of his cuticle and raiment. When his clothes are burned completely off, he counts upon his prudish neighbors for a new garb. Altogether, he is decidedly eccentric even for a madman; and he must be very

mad, for he either refuses money, or, when it is thrust upon
him, tosses it away to other beggars who are always crouching near.

Toward the close of our visit we managed to scrape
acquaintance with the servants of another neighbor. One
was a veiled woman, who would smile at us through her
mask, and another a fat negress slave, as unctuous and good-
natured as any Mississippi mammy. "And are there really
slaves in Fez?" some one may ask. There are ; and every
day in a certain remote and cheerless market-place young
negresses are sold at auction. Seldom, however, does a
stranger witness this trafficking in human flesh. At his
approach, buyers and sellers, slaves and auctioneers, mys-
teriously vanish. Thrice we found the market-place deserted.
Twice, owing to the skillful manœuvering of our guide, we surprised the market in full swing, and saw six little negro girls,

THE PALACE OF A RICH OFFICIAL

AROUND THE MOORISH MAHOGANY

fresh from the barbarous regions of the south, purchased by solemn white-robed citizens at prices varying from eighty to two hundred dollars.

But do not think because our neighbors do not call upon us that we receive no social courtesies whatever. On the contrary, the Minister of Finance, the Moorish Secretary of the Treasury, one of the highest and by a curious coincidence one of the richest dignitaries in Morocco, one day, invited us to dinner. The invitation was delivered through the British vice-consul, who promised to accompany us and to see that we made no *faux pas*. We were not rude enough to take a camera with us, knowing the prejudices of the Moors, and therefore I have no picture of the gorgeous palace into the courtyard of which we were ushered by a group of slaves. Our host resembled the rich men we see daily in the streets, being princely in bearing, haughty and reserved. Contrary to Moorish custom, we sat at a table and on chairs, instead of on the floor. There were no other guests. As soon as we were seated, Mr. MacLeod took from his pocket a paper parcel and opened it, displaying three pairs of knives and forks.

"I always carry these when I dine out with the Moorish swells; they don't have any," he explained; "and they like to have me bring them when they are entertaining foreign guests."

"But how do they eat?" we asked.

"Watch his excellency, and you'll soon understand."

At this moment there appeared a huge round platter, three feet in diameter, on which has been erected a pyramid of chickens. To each of us an entire bird was given. Then our

CARRYING BAKED MEATS TO A FEAST

host, with deft fingers, tore his portion very neatly into shreds, picked out the choicest morsels of the chicken and passed them to us. Then followed pyramids of pigeons, then huge chunks of mutton, then sausages on spits; and that those sausages were not less than two inches thick and one foot long I am positively certain, because we each were compelled to take a whole one, and I remember my vain efforts to get it all upon my plate, three inches of protruding sausage threatening the table-cloth on each side. And every course was carved by our host, who used nothing sharper than his finger-nails, and every time he came upon a morsel of especial daintiness, he courteously offered it to one of us. We were almost stuffed to death, for the consul warned us that to refuse the proffered tidbits would be a great affront. There were no sauces, no vegetables, nothing but meats roasted underground by slow fires that had burned all night.

We had nothing with which to wash down this "all too solid" food except sickly lukewarm rose-water. And not content with stuffing us and forcing us to drink that perfumed liquid, our host would every now and then give a signal, whereupon the servants

"LET ME BE AN AMERICAN FOR A MINUTE!"

THE " MELLAH " OR " GHETTO " OF FEZ

would spray stronger rosewater down our backs and in our ears. Never was anything more welcome than the tiny cups of Turkish coffee that at last were brought to end our tortures. I could not blame my friend, when, on our return to our own house, he declared that he had had enough of Oriental luxury, exclaiming as Haj brought the "antidotes," "Let me be an American for a minute!"

The table was served by two slaves, and by a young man whose bearing told us that he was no servant. He was, in fact, the eldest son of our host. Custom commands that the son should wait upon the father's guests. Imagine this custom introduced at Washington, and picture the sons of a cabinet-official passing huge finger-bowls around the banquet table!

As for our conversation, it turned first upon the only modern institution in the city, the Arsenal and Rifle Factory of the Sultan. The secretary spoke of course in Arabic, the

vice-consul acting as interpreter. Then we were questioned
regarding the city whence we come, Chicago ; and, being
native-born Chicagoans, no urging was required to wring
from us the story of the great phœnix city on the shore of the
American inland sea. We described "skyscrapers," elevat-
ors, cable-cars, and trolleys. Then we told of the World's
Fair, visited in one day by seven times more people than

" A PLACE OF WHITED SEPULCHERS "

reside in Fez, and then with a keener interest the secretary
listened to the incredible figures relating to the movements of
wheat and corn and to the shipments of beef and mutton.
Next, as a climax, we launched enthusiastically into pork
statistics, but our spokesman checks us with the caution:
"Hush ! Don't shock his Excellency ; remember his religious prejudices. Don't say a word about the pigs. You
know the Moslem eats no pork." Therefore we leave our
host unenlightened regarding the pet industry of our western
metropolis.

"AND DINGY HUTS"

The next day we devote to the Jewish quarter, a distinct and separate city, called the "Mellah." We approach it through the Hebrews' burial ground, a place of whited sepulchers, dwellings for the dead, and dingy huts, temporary abodes for living men and women; for there are two populations in the Jewish cemetery, a fixed population of the wealthy dead, a passing population of the living poor. You must remember that in these Moorish cities the Jews are still compelled to dwell apart from true believers. Their houses are confined in the restricted Mellah, where no provision was originally made for an increase of population. Therefore the poorer and the weaker Jews have been squeezed out of its gates and have found refuge here in the city of the dead, where they have built crude huts and begun life anew. The streets or passageways are, however, far cleaner than those of the inner Mellah, and we cannot but agree that residence in

POOR NEIGHBORS OF THE WEALTHY DEAD

the freer atmosphere of this city of the dead is preferable to living on the other side of yonder walls, where every inch of space is occupied, where the atmosphere is heavy with bad odors, and where sunshine and fresh air are things almost unknown.

A poor old Jew, a man with a large dependent family, serves as our guide. He tells of the misery of his people, begs me to repeat in my own land the story of their woe. It

A HOME IN THE CEMETERY

is not the Sultan, he says, who is most cruel to them ; it is the rich men, the elders and the rabbis of his own tribe whom he accuses of injustice.

The right to build these shelters in the cemetery was granted by the Sultan to the poor, when the overcrowding of the Mellah proper became a menace to the public health. Nevertheless, no poor man is permitted to take up his abode among these

THE WALLS OF THE "MELLAH"

cast-out members of the tribe until he has paid certain fees to the headmen of the quarter. He says that the oppression of Jew by Jew is harder to bear than the much-talked-of oppression to which the children of Israel have been subjected by the Sons of Ishmael. The statements of our pauper guide surprised us, but what he said was confirmed by every poor Jew with whom we talked. They all declared that the rich elders and the rabbis of their own tribe were their hardest masters. A wealthy man, with whom we discussed the question later, assured us that his class had almost impoverished itself with charities, that the cause of all the evil lay in the decrease of commerce and the rapid increase of the Jewish population. The poor, undoubtedly, are very poor; and though the rich live in apparent luxury and comfort, it cannot be true that Fez is the only city in the world where the rich Jews abandon their own people to starvation and distress. The noble Jewish charities throughout the world argue the contrary, and even in Fez the philanthropy of European Jews is manifest in the excellent school established here in this very Mellah by the French branch of the Israelite Alliance.

A FOURTEEN-YEAR-OLD MOTHER

We can assure all those who have given pecuniary support to the Alliance that the money is here spent conscientiously, and that the work now doing among the Moorish Jews is nobly done and worthy the sympathy and encouragement of every lover of humanity. But in spite of the educational and civilizing

IN THE MAZE OF REEKING ALLEYS

influences of the school, many reforms in customs remain
to be effected, and it is to be hoped that in the future,
a daughter of the Mellah will not be given in marriage at
the age of ten and, like one girl we saw, be mother of a
family at fourteen years of age, and become at twenty-five
a hideous old woman. Let us hope that in another generation girl-children who at fourteen are still unmarried will
not be regarded, as they are to-day, in the light of hopeless
spinsters.

As for the sanitary reforms demanded in the Mellah, you
have but to enter the crowded streets to be convinced that
they are numberless. Here Jews are packed like live sar-
dines in greasy boxes. Pierre Loti describes the Mellah as
"an airless huddle of houses squeezed together as if screwed
in a compress, and emitting all sorts of stifling odors."

JEWISH COBBLERS

"OLD MEN WHO LOOK THE PART OF SHYLOCK"

Again he tells of finding here "moldy smells in varieties that are not known elsewhere." But how is it possible to expect cleanliness on the part of people who are denied a sufficiency of space and air and light and water, who are not permitted to remove the refuse from their streets, lest the

AN ENGLISH HOME IN FEZ

IN THE MIDST OF THE " MELLAH "

THE FAMILY OF BENSIMON

Moorish scavenger should lose his fee; people who are despised by their Moslem fellow-citizens, called "dogs," and
forced to walk barefooted through the streets of Moorish Fez?

As a crowning indignity, the Moors have decreed that the
place of deposit for dead animals, from cats to camels, shall
be at the gate of the Mellah; and every night the jackals
feast and sing their death chants beneath the walls of this

"IN TINY SHOPS SIT GOLD- AND SILVER-SMITHS"

unhappy Jewish city.   We are surprised, however, to find here and there a touch of color in the dress of these unfortunate inhabitants, for black has always been the uniform imposed upon the Jew.   Black is to Moorish minds the color of disgrace ; hence were the Jews compelled to wear black caps and gaberdines.   To-day, however, this regulation is not so rigidly enforced, although the general tone of the men's dress is very somber.

In every street we see old men, who could, without a change of raiment, step on the theatrical stage and look the part of Shylock to the life.   In tiny shops, like niches bordering these streets, sit the gold- and silver-smiths, the lawyers, scribes, and money-changers ; there are few idlers here.   Jewish industry and thrift here rise superior to the discouraging surroundings.   A few shops boast a supply of foreign merchandise.   The merchants greet us with a polite *"buenos dias,"* and converse in fluent Spanish ; for besides Hebrew and Arabic, these people speak the language of the land from which their fathers were cruelly cast out by Spanish kings.

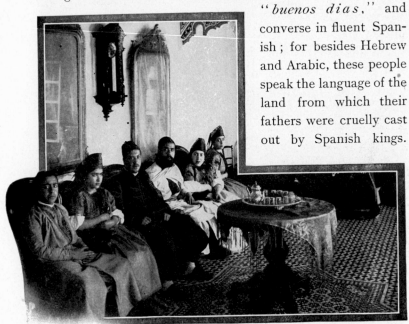

FIVE O'CLOCK TEA IN A HEBREW HOUSEHOLD

The com-
merce of the
land is largely
in the hands of
Moorish Jews,
who are forbid-
den by law to
leave the coun-
try, lest a gen-
eral exodus
occur, and the
trade of the en-
tire empire, de-
prived of their
fostering care,
languish and
ultimately die.
Many large for-
tunes have been

A HEBREW HOME

accumulated here, by usury and commerce. We made a
formal call one Sabbath afternoon at the home of one of the
richest Jews in Fez, old Mr. Bensimon. Magnificent, indeed,
is the interior of the house, with its carved, painted doors,
its stucco arabesques, immaculate tiled floors, and richly
furnished rooms. The Bensimons are of the old conserva-
tives. They speak no Spanish and have no knowledge of
anything away from their immediate surroundings. The
Mellah is their world ; their house is one of the rare oases
of elegance in the midst of a wilderness of squalor. But
they are all very gracious to us ; of the two pretty little girls,
eleven and thirteen years of age, respectively, the elder is
already married, the younger is a fiancée.

A curious incident gave us an insight into the reality of
their religion. To amuse our host we performed some tricks

AT THE SCHOOL OF THE ISRAELITE ALLIANCE

of sleight-of-hand.   Producing a silver dollar, I asked the
aged father to assure himself that it was a real dollar, not
tampered with in any way.   He seemed reluctant to pick up
the coin.

"You must not urge him," said our guide.   "It is the
Jewish Sabbath ; a Jew may not touch filthy lucre on the
holy day."

Before departing we were asked to take tea with the
family, and were forthwith ushered into an apartment, furnished with that crude gaudiness that is the result of Oriental
imitation of Occidental fashions.   Of their "European
Room" they are as proud as we are of our so-called
"Oriental dens."   The mirrors, clocks, sofas, and chande-
liers, imported from the continent, are the envy of their
neighbors.

Tea-drinking in Morocco is a solemn ceremony, to the
stranger almost a sickening one.   A handful of tea is put in
the teapot, and the pot is filled to the very top with sugar,
broken from a huge cone loaf ; then boiling water is poured

on. Then a bouquet of mint is thrust into this saturated
solution of sugar and tea. Next, half a glassful is thrown
away to exorcise evil spirits, and then one glassful is boldly
swallowed by the host to reassure the guests by proving that
there is no intent to poison them. Extravagant as this may
sound, it is a necessary bit of etiquette in a land where tea-
parties are so often fatal to a rich man's enemies. Finally,
little painted glasses full of mint tea are served to all, and
the traditional three rounds of this abominable concoction —
a sort of warm and flat mint-julep, with the true soul of a
mint-julep lacking — must be drunk on pain of being thought
ill-bred. If the glasses are not completely emptied every
time, the residue is complacently turned back into the teapot,
to which more mint and water have meantime been added;

and the greater
noise we make in
drinking the tea,
the better are our
manners thought
to be. The re-
sulting sounds at
a really fashion-
able tea-party
suggest the re-
leasing of the air-
brakes on a rail-
way train.

During the
function, sticky
sweetmeats and
preserved fruits,
that are as revolt-
ing as they are
adhesive, are

"KINDLY FACES SMILING DOWN"

passed repeatedly, and every time we are expected to accept
and eat. I nearly ruined my digestion in an attempt to be
polite. My friend, more happily situated, is able to pour most
of his tea out of the window, and deftly to drop the sticky
abominations out upon the heads of the passers-by.

Escaping finally, we make another call, this time upon
the little colony connected with the mission school of the
French Israelite Alliance. We find it most refreshing to
meet a group of educated people, with whom to talk of all
the strange things we have seen. Among them are the
teachers, sent from France, their wives and families, and also
a number of the most progressive Jews in Fez. The boys
are students of the school, and a fat one is presented as the
prize pupil of the institution, the pride and admiration of his
teachers who put him through his paces at a blackboard

OUR GUESTS

THE PICNIC PARTY IN OUR GARDEN

to convince us of his cleverness. He certainly did gallop
through arithmetical puzzles with rapidity and ease, and
answered the questions that we propounded with a facility
that put us quite to shame, for we could think of nothing difficult enough to stagger him for a moment.

Then, after another infliction of mint tea and some sweetmeats that seemed like sugar-coated sausages, we take our
leave, descend the narrow stair-
way, and pass out into the
dingy little street. An avalanche of shouts and laugh-
ter overwhelms us, and

ISRAELITE SOCIETY IN FEZ

looking up we see the sky-line of the house adorned with
a border of kindly faces, smiling down a cheery "*au revoir.*"
For it has been arranged that we are all to meet again upon
the morrow. These new-found friends have been invited to
spend the day at our villa, to attend a picnic in our garden,
to forget, there in the leafy spaciousness of our temporary
abode, the cramped and airless houses of the Mellah.

"EVERYWHERE THE
SOUND OF RUNNING WATER"

There are no private gardens in the Mellah, lack of space forbids ; nor are there public gardens in the Moorish city. Therefore the Jews must take their air and sunshine on the housetops, where level terraces, surrounded by low parapets, afford them opportunities to bake themselves in the torrid atmosphere of Africa. Needless to say, our invitation was accepted, and next morning, shortly after breakfast, a caravan of white-robed guests makes its appearance at our garden door. The women have ridden on mule-back across the city, for they are all protégés of France, and therefore are not compelled to go about on foot, like nearly all their co-religionists.

Great preparations have been made by Haj for their entertainment. He has adorned the house and court-yard with objects borrowed from unsuspecting owners. Let me explain that almost every evening when we return from rambles in the city, we find awaiting us two or three dealers in curios, rugs, old brocades, and Moorish weapons ; their goods spread out in a most artistic, tempting fashion. Haj has induced the men who came the night before to leave

their goods on approval until the following evening ; and thus
it is that we are able to give our picnic a rich Oriental setting without incurring any great expense.   In the picture of
the merrymakers it may be interesting to identify my friend,
who sits on the extreme left, robed in a white burnoose.
Then on the right is Haj, dressed in his best ; near him there
sits an old gray-bearded man.   He is our only Moorish guest,
one of the few Moors who is free from the prejudices of his
race, who does not fear to sit at meat with Jews and Christians ; moreover, he speaks Spanish fluently.   But he is
more of a good fellow than a good Mohammedan ; to our
knowledge he dares to disregard the rule of total abstinence
imposed upon the nation, for in his home there is a secret
cellar filled with wine.   And, curiously, this old *bon vivant*,
who to-day makes merry with us in our Moorish garden,
bears the same name as he who sang the joys of the jug in a
Persian garden long ago ; his name, too, is Omar.

Our guests remain with us from morning until evening,
departing just before the hour when the great wooden gates

"NOTHING REMINISCENT OF THE CITIES OF OUR WORLD"

of every district are closed securely for the night.   In Fez,
the populace keeps early hours.   After nine o'clock it is
impossible to enter or to leave the city or even to pass from
one quarter to another, be it adjacent or remote.   The gates
once closed, each district is completely isolated, and all who
are shut in must wait till morning to escape ; all who are
shut out must spend the night away from home, unless they
be men of influence, or carry written orders for the opening
of the barriers.   There is, of course, nothing to do at night ;
there are no theaters, clubs, or evening parties ; the city life
dies out at sunset.   The people go to their homes before the
gates are closed.   There is by night no movement save the

THE STREET THAT SKIRTS
OUR GARDEN WALL

flowing of the waters.
A river sings its way
through the heart of
Fez, and swift canals
are laughing in every
quarter.   There is
everywhere in Fez
the sound of running
water, as in Rome,
as at Nikko in Japan,
as round the hill of
the Alhambra.   The
sound is thus asso-
ciated in my mind
with four of the most
fascinating places in
the world.   There is
not in the entire city
a building that is
reminiscent of the
cities of our world ;
there is no smoke,

"NAUGHT IN COMMON WITH THE COMMERCE OF TO-DAY"

and there are no chimneys ; there are no vehicles of any kind
in Fez, there is but one wheeled vehicle in the whole Empire ; it is the state-coach given by Queen Victoria to the
Sultan, a curiosity that is exhibited on state occasions, but a
turnout in which the Sultan never rides.   There is no noise

" ROOFLESS DUNGEONS THAT SERVE AS STREETS "

in Fez — no noise as we understand the word ; there are
sounds, pleasant and unpleasant, but the ceaseless roar of
western cities is not there.   The struggle for existence is
almost a silent struggle.   Moreover, I believe that Fez is
in a higher state of civilization, and that its people are less
given to crime than are the dwellers in the poorer quarters of
London, Paris, and New York.   It is safe for a Moorish

citizen to walk these crowded streets by day ; at night he
sleeps securely in his home.   There is no flagrant immorality.
yet there is no regular police.

The streets of Fez can never cease to astonish men from
the modern world.   We may have seen similar settings on
the stage, similar costumes in pictures or museums ; so these
are not new to us.   What astonishes us is that these things
should anywhere form a part of the actual daily life of men
and women of our own time.   And this life does not even
touch our life ; its points of contact with the outside world
are few.   Commercial Fez communicates with the mysterious
regions of the south, with Senegambia and Timbuctu, by
means of camel fleets that traverse seas of sand.   This com-

"THERE IS NO NOISE IN FEZ"

Photograph by Nelson Ludington Barnes

THE SACRED HOUR OF MOGHREB

merce has naught in common with the commerce of our world ; its methods and its means of transport are totally

foreign to our own, and its itineraries are far beyond
our ken.

But this city that appears so dim and so mysterious as we
walk through the roofless dungeons that serve as streets,
reveals to us a brilliant, dazzling aspect, when, disregarding
the unwritten law forbidding men to go upon housetops, we

OUR LAST EVENING IN FEZ

venture out upon the terrace of our villa. The roof terraces
are sacred to the women ; there they may bare their faces in
the light of day, there they may lay aside their shrouds, and,
bathed in the soft evening light, appear for a brief space as
living women,— women with charms and personalities. The
men of Fez have tacitly agreed that on the housetops the
women shall be free from male observation, free to forget
that they are practically slaves. We could not bind our-

WHERE UNBELIEVERS SELDOM TREAD

selves to keep this courteous law, the view from our roof
terrace was too tempting.   All Fez was there spread out before
us, Fez with its snowy dwellings reflecting the golden rays of
the declining sun, Fez with its minarets, its mosques, its
palaces ; Fez with its streets seldom trodden by the feet of unbelievers, its sacred places never polluted by an alien glance.

"THE FIERCE SURROUNDING COUNTRY"

Old Fez so long the city of our dreams, now become
the city of our waking thoughts, is soon to become the
city of our reminiscences.   For alas! this is to be our
last evening in the holy city.   The limit of official tolerance
is reached ; our passports have been suggestively returned,
and, knowing the futility of protest, we dine in regretful
silence close to the open window that we may not lose a
single phase of the ever-changing coloring and lighting of the
picture there revealed to us.   For the last time we watch the
city grow dim in the twilight ; although we have witnessed

ten times the dying of the day from this same window,
the spectacle has not lost its charm, the picture has not lost
its fascinating mystery. A sojourn of ten days in Fez has
not dissipated, it has but deepened the sense of mystery.
But we, to our surprise, have not yet suffered from that
strange mental disease, the "longing to get away" that
infallibly attacks ambassadors and representatives of foreign
powers and is a political force upon which Moorish diplomats
may count to rid them of annoying visitors who have come
to press vexing demands upon their government. At last a
sudden glow, like a great flood of fire, overspreads the city ;
it is the glow of sunset, the last signal of the dying day, and
for a moment it suffuses the entire heavens, as if there were
a distant world in conflagration. Fez has assumed a shroud
of black ; it is the sacred hour of Moghreb, and the lower
darkness is resounding with the cries of the Muezzin, those
cries of intense faith, those wailing laments that seem to
express the nothingness of all things earthly.

The Moors speak of their country as " Moghreb-al-Aksa, "
the " Country of the Setting Sun." How prophetic !—for
in very truth the sun of civilization has set forever upon this
land, and though its past be brilliant as the heavenly sunset
fires, its future is as dim as the soft-footed night that, steal-
ing in from the black, fierce surrounding country, broods like
a pall of death above the sleeping city of the Moors.

THROUGH THE HEART OF THE MOORISH EMPIRE

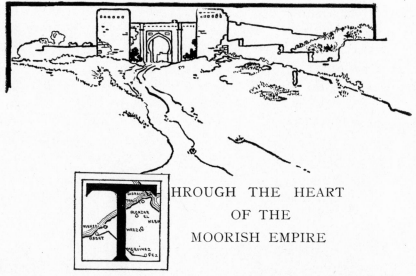

THROUGH THE HEART
OF THE
MOORISH EMPIRE

THE spell of mystery is still upon Morocco. The Moors are still the people of romance. Of the land we know comparatively little ; of the race as it exists to-day we know still less. Christendom assumes that the Moorish Empire expired with the last sigh of Boabdil, leaving the Alhambra as its only legacy.

Almost novel is the thought that the Moors still live as a nation ; that Morocco is to-day what Spain would have become had the forces of the Prophet prevailed in the Peninsula. Who would not welcome as a precious privilege the possibility of turning back the pages of history in Spain, to revel in the actual Moorish life as it was lived before the Christian victories of 1492 ? Who would not gladly leave, at least for a short space, the familiar round of present-day

existence and the hackneyed paths of travel, to plunge into a
past so picturesque, to see a civilization so refined and yet so
utterly unlike our own ? No reader of Washington Irving
but has longed to people with white-clad cavaliers the courts
on the Alhambra Hill, to hear the Arab accents in the streets
of old Granada, or the murmuring of the Moslem prayers in
the old mosques. But why persist in holding Spain to be
the sole stage on which the Moors appropriately can play
their parts ?

Morocco was their home ere Spain was conquered for
them. When Andalusia ungratefully cast out the race that
brought it light and knowledge at a time when Europe groped
in the blackness of deep ignorance, back to Morocco went
the Empire of the Moors. Empires rise and fall. The
Moorish Empire rose but did not fall ; it was shaken but not
shattered ; it is still erect. It stands a living skeleton wrapt
in the shroud of Islam, its hollowness concealed by the vague

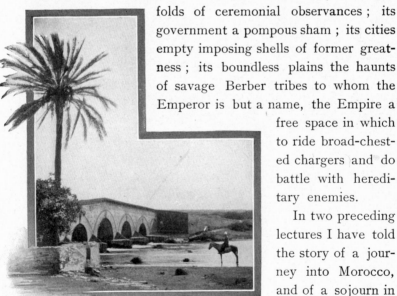

folds of ceremonial observances ; its
government a pompous sham ; its cities
empty imposing shells of former greatness ; its boundless plains the haunts
of savage Berber tribes to whom the
Emperor is but a name, the Empire a
free space in which
to ride broad-chest-
ed chargers and do
battle with heredi-
tary enemies.

In two preceding
lectures I have told
the story of a jour-
ney into Morocco,
and of a sojourn in

ON THE ROAD TO MEQUINEZ Fez, the metropolis

DIGNITARIES *EN VOYAGE*

of the Moors. There yet remains to tell a third, conclud-
ing chapter of the tale — the narrative of the return from
Fez to the sea, from a remote yesterday back to the world of
to-day. " Out of Morocco " would serve as an appropriate
heading for this chapter, — a chapter rich in adventure and
in picturesque experiences. For ten days we have dwelt in

BRIDGES COMPETE UNSUCCESSFULLY WITH FORDS

medieval Moslem Fez — unwelcome visitors, objects of suspicion to the jealous Moors.

Two routes are open to us — the direct road to Tangier
and the less-frequented road to Rabat on the Atlantic Coast.
Despite the protest of the authorities, who warn us of many
dangers, we chose the road that leads westward to Mequinez,
the Beni-Hasan Plain, and the Atlantic. But the word
" road " must be regarded only in its Moroccan sense. As

has been said already, there are no roads in this wild land ;
the slow caravans and the swift troops of Moorish horsemen
have followed the hoofmarks left by the caravans or troops

MIDWAY BETWEEN FEZ AND MEQUINEZ

which have preceded them, until a system of narrow trails
meandering in uncertain parallels has been created between
the inland cities and the sea.

These Moorish highways were never surveyed and never
tended ; like Topsy — who, also, by the way, was an African
product — they were never born, "they just growed ;" and
like Topsy they are wilfully unreasonable ; they exasperate
us by their defiance of conventionality ; amuse us with their
peculiar antics, and delight us with preposterous surprises.

As an example, take the highway that leads from Fez to
the neighboring city of Mequinez. As we approach a river,

the wandering trails converge and form a beaten track that grows more and more like a real road as it winds down toward a substantial bridge. But just as we are about to compliment the road on its reform, it suddenly grows weary of good behavior, becomes rebellious, and, like a balky mule, refuses to cross the bridge. Incredible as it may seem to those who do not know this land of contradictions, Moorish roads will not cross Moorish rivers by means of Moorish bridges. The old way is preferred. Fording was good enough in the old days, and it is good enough to-day. The roads turn sharply from the bridge abutments, scramble down the muddy banks, and plunge into the yellow rivers to emerge slimy and dripping on the opposite shore. The bridges, ponderously useless, studiously neglected, are falling into decay, and have become almost impassable.

We pitch our camp not far from one of those disdained reminders of an attempt at progress. We are midway between Fez and Mequinez in a region notorious because of the thieving bands with which it is infested. It appears

MIDDAY REPOSE

wholly unpeopled ; yet we are not without misgivings, for, of our caravan, four mules and two men have gone astray. With us are Haj, the dragoman, Achmedo, the valet, and the muleteers, Abuktayer and Bokhurmur. The missing are Kaid Lharbi, the military escort, and the new packer who joined our force in Fez. We have our tent and Haj's kitchen ; the other tents and all the supplies and furniture are in the packs of the missing mules somewhere on this gloomy plain, possibly already become the loot of some lawless sheik, or, as we hope, merely delayed because of broken harness, or gone astray because of a mistaken trail. Our groundless fears are set at rest an hour later by the safe arrival of the precious convoy, and once more our palates are delighted by the delicious dinner cooked by Haj, our thirst quenched by cooled oranges, and our weary bodies laid to rest upon our comfortable camp-cots.

WIFE, CHILD, AND SLAVE

After the con-
finement incident
to our residence
in city quarters,
the free life of the
plains is doubly
exhilarating, and
we find intense
pleasure in the
satisfaction of
the simple, keen
desires to eat,
drink, and sleep.
All food is good,
all drink is bet-
ter, sleep the
sweetest gift of
the gods.

"YO SOY CHINO, SEÑOR"

The morning
finds us early in the saddle ; four hours' westward progress brings us at noon to one of those rare oases of
shadow in this bare land of sunshine.   Here hunger, thirst,
and weariness are again assuaged by food and drink and
sleep. Sharp darts of brilliant, blinding sunshine burn
through the leafy masses of the two fig-trees, and with
almost malicious persistence pursue the would-be slumberer,
who, to avoid this, must every now and then crawl after the
receding shadows.

But we are not the only travelers who have sought midday shelter in this forest.   On our approach we were greeted
by a family group, — a man and woman with a little child,
and a black slave.   To our surprise the man addressed us in
Spanish : —

  "*Buenos dias, Señor, habla usted Español ?*"

"*Si, Señor, un poco,*" we reply, and then begins an interesting conversation.

"Where are your animals?" we ask.

"Stolen with all my goods, last night," he answers. "We must now go on foot to Fez to report our loss to the authorities."

We learn that our unfortunate friend is a maker of sausage cases, that he lives in Mequinez, and that he is hospitably inclined; for in return for our sympathy, he begs us to make use of his house in Mequinez, where another of his wives will welcome us and give us food and lodging.

OUR DUSKY CHARGE

This strange offer of hospitality, coupled with a something in the man's expression leads me to say, "But, Señor, you are not like a Moor."

"Why should I be?" he smilingly asks. "*Yo, yo soy Chino.*" "I, I am a Chinese."

WALLS THAT DO NOT KEEP EVEN THE SUNSHINE OUT

He is the nappy father of a dainty little girl, a type of
Chinese beauty, and two lusty boys, who bear upon their
faces maps of Peking and Canton. The negress, his slave,
he is sending back to Mequinez with tidings of his loss. Haj,

MULAI ISMAIL'S WALL

with Occidental gallantry, offers the dusky damsel his place
on a pack-mule, and after the exchange of many kindnesses
our little company, made up of individuals so diverse in race,
in language, and in thought, breaks up.

Our Chinese Moor with wife and child go trudging off
toward Fez, while the American caravan with its Arab escort
and African passenger moves toward the other great interior
city, Mequinez. Long before we come in sight of Mequinez,
we find our progress barred by a huge wall forty feet or more
in height, stretching away in two directions as far as the eye

WANDERING WALLS

can reach.   But there are ogive archways, through which our caravan passes as freely as the sunshine or the breeze.   There are no gates, no guards, to hinder us. On we file across vacant fields until we reach a second wall as forbidding as the first and apparently as interminable.

" What are these walls ? " we ask.   " Why were they built ? what purpose can they serve ? "

And Haj tells us that they were reared to protect the city from the turbulent surrounding tribes, to cut off, if need be, the approach of hostile bands.

A third wall, wide and high, beginning at the city gate wanders away toward the south, its utility not easily divined. As we trace its curving course over a distant ridge, we think of the Roman aqueducts in the Campagna, and of the great wall of China, for this unknown Moorish work vies with those famous masses of masonry in impressiveness of aspect if not in hugeness and in length of years.   It was the creation of the crazy Sultan, Mulai Ismail, a contemporary of Louis XIV, of France, a Moorish emperor who suffered from a mania for masonry, and made his people suffer that he might satisfy his madness for works of colossal inutility.

One of his wildest projects was the building of an elevated boulevard, two hundred miles in length, along which he could ride from Mequinez to Morocco City, safe from the attack of the rebellious tribesmen who hold the intervening provinces.

The huge north gate of this his favored city appears to us as we approach late in the afternoon like the entrance to some "mysterious nowhere." It seems to be a portal to the empty sky, a door through which the traveler might pass into the infinity of space. It is, in fact, the gate of an almost deserted metropolis, a city that was built for a population of one hundred thousand and contains to-day less than six thousand souls. Small wonder that we find it empty and forsaken in aspect as we pass from court to court and through gate after gate. There are in Mequinez more houses vacant than occupied, more roofs fallen than intact, more palaces in ruins than huts in good repair. The Sultan is forced to maintain a palace here, for Mequinez ranks with

LIKE THE PORTAL TO A "MYSTERIOUS NOWHERE"

16

THE SULTAN'S PALACE — MEQUINEZ

Fez and Morocco City as one of the three capitals of the Moorish Empire, each city jealous of its dignity as the abode of the Imperial master.

The Sultan always dwells amid the wreck of ages. The snow-white palace of the actual sovereign may be seen rising above the crumbling walls of the Imperial Garden. Around

"THROUGH GATE AFTER GATE"

Photograph by Neison Ludington Barnes
'BORN OF AN IMPERIAL MANIA FOR MASONRY"

it are vague piles of age-worn masonry, the abandoned palaces of emperors who ruled here in the past.   Custom
demands that on the death of a Sultan his palace be abandoned and a new one built for his successor.   It is regarded
as a sacrilege for any one to occupy the abode of a departed
emperor.   Thus, during the centuries, these imperial inclos-

ures in all the Moorish cities have become encumbered with acres of decaying palaces in which bats and owls hold carnival.

In Mequinez everything speaks of Mulai Ismail, the tyrant Sultan of the seventeenth century, that imperial monster whose deeds surpass in horror those of Nero or Caligula, the ruins

AN ARTIFICAL LAKE

of whose palaces and public works rival in magnitude the Roman mountains of brick and stone upon the Palatine or in the broad Campagna.

Mulai Ismail built three miles of stables for his twelve thousand horses. We see, to-day, the endless aisles of arches where his chargers were lodged in splendor, every ten horses tended by a negro slave. As a horseman, he was superb. It is said that he was able, in one graceful movement, to

ENDLESS AISLES OF ARCHES

mount his steed, draw his sword, and neatly decapitate the slave who held his stirrup. He held that to die by his imperial hand insured immediate entry into paradise, and throughout the latter part of his life of eighty-one vigorous years he went about his land dispensing, with his scimitar, passports to a beatitudinous eternity. Twenty thousand of his subjects were thus favored, Friday being the day chosen by the imperial murderer for these execution-ary exer- cises. His pet lions were fed

upon the slaves; his were treated children, though flesh of forty cats better than his one disobedient

OUR CAMP IN THE KASBAH

cat was formally executed by his order. Workmen caught idling on the walls, at which his myriad slaves and prisoners were unceasingly engaged, were tumbled into the molds and rammed down into the concrete.

An incredibly atrocious deed crowned his career of crime. A wife suspected of infidelity was filled with powder and blown to pieces. The mere drowning of a wife in the small artificial lake was but a gentle pastime. He had two

thousand wives.   As to the number of his children we must
accept the word of an ambassador of Louis XIV, who visited
the court of Mulai Ismail in 1703.   He asked the favorite
son how many brothers and sisters he possessed.   After two
days spent in compiling a catalogue, the Prince submitted
the names of five hundred and twenty-five brothers and three
hundred and forty-two sisters.   Later reports give the number of sons who lived to mount horse the astounding total of
seven hundred.   To create palaces and to people them was
the life-work of Mulai Ismail.

One incident that makes this impossible man seem real to
us is this : He actually sent ambassadors to France to demand
of Louis XIV the hand of Mlle. de Blois, the natural daughter of the King and Louise de la Vallière !   The honor was
declined in polite terms by the Grand Monarque.

THE GATE OF KASBAH — MEQUINEZ

In Mulai's day Europeans were not
strangers to Morocco ; but they came —
not as we come to-day, as travelers with
tents and guides to camp freely for a few
sunny days under the imperial walls —
they came as slaves and captives taken
from merchant-ships by pirates ; they
came with chains and manacles, to toil
for dark, hopeless years in building these
same walls, in piling up these useless
miles of mud, brick, and cement. The
thought of the sufferings endured
by them makes doubly strange our
actual comfort ; the dangers of the
living past throw into striking contrast the security of the dead present. We are not even annoyed by

STUDYING THE STRANGERS

crowds. Perhaps there are no crowds in Mequinez to-day.
The only citizen who deigns to take an interest in us is an old
man who rides up on a tiny donkey and sits studying the
strangers with a plainly puzzled look upon his wrinkled face.
That he may not depart without some mark of our apprecia-
tion of his call, we display our modern arsenal, a shotgun and
a rifle, testing the latter by firing at an eagle that is soaring
overhead. By chance the shot is a successful one. Down
comes the big bird like a meteorite, grazing the donkey's ear,
and falling with a thud at his astonished nose ; whereupon
our visitor having seen enough rides off in silence to tell of
our prowess in the half-deserted bazaars.

From Mequinez we carry away impressions as enduring as
its walls and gates. We know that we shall never forget the
sadness of this empty city, its silence, and its forlorn magnifi-
cence. In all Morocco there is no more artistic structure
than the Kasbah Gate of Mequinez. It is as it was ; no

restoration has marred it.   Time has but softened it, made it
more beautiful.   Corinthian pillars, brought from the ruins of
the Roman city of Volubilis, add to its dignity and tell of a
civilization that long antedates that of the Arab conquerors.
It, too, like every gate and every palace in the city of Mulai
Ismail recounts its tragedy.   The man whose mind conceived

GOOD SHOOTING IN THE HEART OF THE CITY

its form, its intricate designs, its unsymmetrical perfections,
fell victim to his artist-pride.   For, when the Sultan com-
plimented him on his achievements, he declared that he could
build a gate more beautiful, more imposing, did the imperial
master so desire ; and this boast cost the architect his eyes,
for the Sultan was resolved that this, his favorite gate, should
have no rival and no peer.   Less beautiful, but more imposing is the great North Gate by which we enter and through
which we ride out into the black, treacherous country.   Our

A THOROUGHFARE IN MEQUINEZ

THE BENI-HASAN PLAIN

muleteers have halted at a fountain to drink and pray ; for
the fountain marks the burial-place of a great Moslem saint,
the founder of the fraternity of the Hamdouchi, a kindred
society to that of the fanatical Aissaoua, a sect of self-tor-
turers and religious maniacs.

Devotions ended, the caravan
reforms, and we find our-
selves trailing across an
empty land, which we
have been warned on
no account to enter.
Two days of un-
eventful travel over
the hills of a rolling
region brings us to
the brink of the in-
terior highland, from
which we look down
upon the level plain that
stretches westward to the wide

THE NORTH GATE
OF MEQUINEZ

A SOKO IN THE WILDERNESS

Atlantic, many miles away. Below us lies the country of the famous Beni-Hasan tribe. The "Sons of Hasan" are famous as horsemen, warriors, and pirates of the plain. Our route lies westward across their territory to the seaport city called Rabat, where we hope to embark in due time on one of the infrequent coasting-steamers that ply up and down the western coast of Africa.

As we descend the steep trail winding down from the hill region, we look in vain for any sign of town or village. A few clumps of dark green trees and yellow streams are all that break the dull monotony of the wide vista,— all, save a patch of gray, which looks at first like a heap of rags spread out for an airing and a sunning. But as we draw nearer to it, we observe that the rag-pile is alive, that it swarms and moves in slow confusion. Each rag enwraps a human-being ; there are at least a thousand of them come together

in this desert-place to buy and barter food and drink
and raiment.

A curious feature of commerce in Morocco are these fairs
held periodically in chosen localities, far from any settlement
or village. A few days later this spot, now the scene of picturesque activity, will be brooded over by the silence and
desolation of the surrounding plain. It will remain unvisited
until, at the advent of another fair, the people of the broad
region roundabout will come again to this townless market-
place, with cattle, fruits and vegetables, woolen goods and
Manchester cotton, old flintlock muskets and inlaid Moorish
daggers, to meet their fellow-merchants, to haggle with crafty
customers, and to indulge that desire for social intercourse,
innate even in the forgotten people of this empty, lonely land.

We spend an hour or two at this Soko in the wilderness,
watching the ant-hill-like activity of the gray-clad sons of
Hasan. The water-sellers do a thriving business, for the sun
beats down relentlessly on this unsheltered mart. From
tented restaurants are wafted odors which may be appetizing
to the native epicure. The butchers are at their work out in

A TOWNLESS MARKET-   PLACE

WATER
BY
THE
CUPFUL

the full glare of the midday sun. There is but little delay between the abattoir and the pot or frying-pan. In fact, the fresh meat might almost be broiled without the aid of any fire whatever when the sun is high and hot.

It is but natural that we should be objects of curiosity, but so reserved and proud are the Moslems that even in this remote place they refrain from paying us the compliment of popular attention. We are neither courted nor insulted. Indifferent glances are all that they vouchsafe us. Whatever of hostility they feel toward the " dog of a Christian " is vented upon our servants. A man attempted to steal a knife from Haj. Haj strikes at him, the crowd sides with the would-be thief, and begins to rain blows upon our guide and muleteers, but they defend themselves until lazy Kaid Lharbi can be induced to make haste slowly to the rescue. The appearance of our soldier quells the tumult. The dispute is referred to a young sheik of the tribe, who, as one in authority, listens to our story and to the clamor of the crowd, and like a righteous judge, orders Haj's assailant put in chains. Before leaving, in order to propitiate the crowd, we beg the sheik to release the culprit. This done, we depart amid approving murmurs.

Just before sunset we reach a narrow, turbid river. There is no bridge. Our pack-mules glissade down the slippery bank and trudge unhesitatingly across the shallow ford. Fortunately, we have crossed the many rivers without inconvenience ; but had we entered Morocco a month earlier, while the rivers are swollen by the April rain, we should have

"AS ONE IN AUTHORITY"

suffered tedious and dangerous delays at every ford. The yellow flood respects not even the caravans of ambassadors and ministers. Official pack-mules have been swept away, official bedding soaked in Moorish rivers, and many a diplomat traveling in state to Fez on some important mission has been compelled to doff his uniform and dignity, and to breast the turgid waters of the River Sebu or the Wad Makhazan. Half regretting that we are deprived of similar experiences, we ride on till we reach a place called Bogari, where we apply for the protection of the kaid of the village. The traveler should lose no time in taking advantage of the laws of hospitality. In them he finds his surest safeguard. The person and property of a guest are sacred. A robber Kaid becomes an ideal host, answering for your safety with his life,

APPETIZING ODORS

FRESH MEAT

guarding your property better than he guards his own.   But
the very man who shelters you one night may, on the morrow, after you have passed beyond the territory for the peace
of which he is held responsible, swoop down upon your caravan with a cloud of gaily arrayed followers and seize such of
your possessions as may have attracted his fancy while you
were enjoying his protection.   By so doing he also gets the
neighboring chieftain into hot water, for failing to protect
you.   Our official letters from the Moorish authorities at
Tangier command all Kaids and Bashas to give us hospitality
and protection and, when necessary, to provide an escort for
our safe-conduct across their respective territories.

Kaid Absalam of Bogari is pleased to order our camp
pitched in his front-yard.   We should have preferred an isolated site beyond the village amid the freshness and the flowers of the plain, but we feel more secure under the eaves of
the official residence, a mud-brick hut, with disheveled thatch.

Kaid Absalam grants us the use of his front-yard, including the dirt, dust, and flies, imposing only one condition upon us. He has been informed by men familiar with the ways of Christians that they invariably travel with "picture-making boxes," or "painting machines," with which they do sinfully and wilfully break the Mosaic commandment, "Thou shalt not make unto thyself the likeness of any living thing." The Kaid's will is that if we possess such inventions of the devil, we shall religiously refrain from using them in his domain.

In this emergency we turn to Haj Abd-er-Rahman Salama, for we know him to be the most artistic prevaricator in Morocco. He rises to the occasion. Never was a village more thoroughly photographed than Bogari, never were a Kaid and a community more blissfully unconscious that crime was rampant under their very noses. Haj presents us formally as two great American astronomers traveling in Morocco on a scientific mission. The Moors of old prided themselves upon their knowledge of the heavens. Astronomy is still in high esteem. The Kaid begs us to display our astronomical instruments. We promptly unpack and set up two photographic-cameras, and arm ourselves with kodaks. One by one, or

NEARING THE LAND OF
THE BENI-HASAN

rather three by three, the dignified villagers put their heads
beneath the focusing cloth, from the black folds of which
come smothered exclamations of delight as they behold upon
the glass inverted images of familiar forms and faces.

Meantime we are " taking the altitude of the sun " with
kodaks. The result of our first attempt shows an African

IN THE SHEIK'S " FRONT YARD "

" son " black as an eclipse ; there are wooly prominences
on the disk, and several satellites are visible. A second
experiment reveals a young Phœbus Apollo, dark as Pluto,
and almost as naked as Eros. Later observations show the
constellation of Venus shedding the light of smiles upon this
land of darkness.

Meantime my friend wins popularity with the ladies of
the galaxy by performing a series of simple tricks of sleight-

"A PLACE CALLED BOGARI"

of-hand.   He catches money in the air, or pretends to find it
in their veils or sleeves.

FORDING

Encouraged by his success, I bring into play the skill acquired in my schoolboy days, when Hermann, not Stoddard, was the man whose career appeared most tempting to me. I, too, win smiles of surprise and wonder-struck expressions from the simple folk of Bogari by swallowing coins and corks, performing card-tricks, or picking pennies from the folds of ragged garments. The last trick is the most popular, for the pennies are invariably claimed by those from whom they have been plucked into visibility. Fond mothers bring forward several lots of Berber babies, and present them, one by one, to the magician, that he may deftly extract the latent wealth from their scant clothing.

THE KAID AND THE CAMERA

But not only did we succeed in fooling the fledglings and the female birds, our magic powers won us the respect and reverence even of the grim, hawk-like cavaliers. We gave a matinée for the Kaid and his chief men. They were deeply impressed and murmured compliments with bated breath; for that which he cannot understand the Moor

Photograph by
Neison Ludington Barnes INSPECTING "ASTRONOMICAL" INSTRUMENTS

regards as supernatural.   The man with occult powers is to be feared, respected, and propitiated.   We had not counted upon this; but Haj, the clever rascal who was under contract to furnish all provisions for our larder, encouraged us thereafter to give daily performances, for every performance elicited substantial tokens of respect in the form of chickens, baskets of eggs, haunches of fine mutton, pails of goats' milk, and plates of honey.

Our reputation as conjurors once established, Haj paid out

ALMOST A "COON"

no more money to the villagers, exacting everywhere a willing tribute or "mouna" from the Sheiks or Kaids.

But one more achievement crowned our perfidy to the kind people of Bogari. The Kaid bade us take tea in his mud-house the night before our departure. We donned our Moorish jelabas, and at the appointed hour sat with the Hasan tribemen around the steaming samovar — for the Russian samovar is the "*grand luxe*" of even the pettiest of chieftains. The situation was rich in its appeal to our love of things remote and strange. Here were we, robed in white garments made by the tailors of Fez, crouching on mats, sipping sweetened mint-tea in company with men of Berber blood, whose profession is plunder, whose relaxation is battle. The Kaid's brother lies prostrate, undergoing a rough massage treatment to allay the pain caused by bullet-wounds received in a recent foray. Grim visaged retainers peer in at the door, keen eyes flash in the outer darkness. The candle flickers, the samovar sings softly, now and then a word is spoken, and a few seconds later a guttural reply is heard, or a grunt of pain from the wounded warrior breaks the hush of the assembly.

Resolved that this scene must be pictured, I appeal to Haj to put his powers of prevarication once more to the test — to lie us into a favorable opportunity for discharging one of our flash-lights here and now.

A REAL AFRICAN

A FLASH OF "MIDNIGHT SUNSHINE"

He hesitates. Dare he attempt another fabrication? Success has made him bold. He speaks, "Oh, Kaid, my masters the astronomers, to whose skill your village can bear witness, ask of you one more favor. To-morrow they set out across our unknown country. To lay their course across this wide land without roads they must take observation of the sun by night as well as by day. At their command the

POPULAR WITH THE LADIES

sun will pierce the veil of night. Permit them once more to set up their instruments, and they will cause the brightness of the orb of day to flash for a brief instant even here between the four walls, beneath thy roof.''

Allured by the promise of this miracle, the Kaid consents. The cameras are placed. The flash-powder is spread. Then with impressive gestures I invoke the god of day, and Haj ignites the fuse.

A great light fills the chamber, clouds form and roll out into the night, the sons of Hasan gasp and murmur prayers.

Photograph by Nelson Ludington Barnes
LOTS OF BERBER BABIES

The astronomers calmly sit down and figure out their reckon-
ing, and lay the course for the caravan voyage for the morrow.
No suspicion rested on us. Kaid Absalam next day escorted
us to the confines of his territory, and thanked us for having
kept our pledge not to paint pictures
of his people.

Photograph by Nelson Ludington Barnes
FOOLING THE FLEDGLINGS

Our caravan files westward across the plain, which is as peaceful as a summer sea. We traverse patches of color, bigger than townships, where the earth is steeped in the crimson of anemones, or the yellow of buttercups. At midday, while the sun hangs almost in the zenith, and the mules trample on their own shadows at every step, an incident breaks the monotony of our ever

TIDINGS OF TROUBLE

silent progress. A solitary man appears on the horizon, his hooded head the only thing that rises above the level of the weeds and flowers. At last he comes within hailing distance, and we exchange greetings. He is a courier, bearing dispatches to Mequinez. He speaks excitedly to Haj, who listens to his words with visible anxiety, for he conveys tidings of trouble from the west. It is the old story of inter-tribal hostilities, of Beni-Zimour razzias in the Beni-Hasan plain, of Beni-Hasan retaliatory trips into the hill-country of the Beni-Zimour. The village of Twazit, where we

THE IMPERIAL POST

KAID ABSALAM

intend to spend the night, was attacked early this very morning, the Beni-Zimour troop was driven off, the Beni-Hasan horsemen have been called out to defend their frontier. We press on rapidly until we meet a company of cavaliers led by the young Kaid of Twazit, who is scouring the country to assemble all the available fighting men. He halts our caravan and demands to know our destination and the purpose of our journey. He forbids our advance into the disturbed region, being responsible to the central government for our safety. But seeing picturesque possibilities in the adventure, we insist upon our right to official protection, and Haj demands an escort for us. The Kaid cannot refuse. Eight men are detached from his troop and detailed for escort-duty. With eagerness we ride on toward the seat of war, if war be not too dignified a name for one of these periodic inter-tribal squabbles.

Peace is upon the plain, calm is in the air ; yet danger and suspicion ride with us, and point across the flowery expanse toward the dark line far to the south,— a line that indicates the wooded country of the Zimour tribe, which holds the region between Mequinez and the southern capital city, Marrakesh (or, as it appears on many maps, Morocco City).

WESTWARD UNDER ESCORT

So successfully have the Beni-Zimour held the Sultan's troops at bay that it has never been possible for the Imperial master, even with the usual escort of thirty thousand men, to march by the direct route from city to city. He has always been forced to go around the very heart of his own empire, to cross this plain to Rabat, thence travel down the coast, and finally strike inland along the southern boundary of the

AN ANXIOUS MOMENT

"PEERING ACROSS THE PLAIN"

possessions of his rebellious subjects.   Thus every state-progress
from one of his capitals to the
other becomes a public hu-
miliation of Morocco's ruler,
whose boast is that his throne
is his horse's saddle, his
canopy the sky, his palace
the great tent in which he
spends more than half of
every year.

The Beni-Hasan, while
none too loyal to the Sultan
in the season when he sends
to them his Bashas to col-
lect the taxes, are hereditary

PICTURESQUE PROTECTORS

TOWARD THE SETTING SUN

enemies of their rebellious neighbors, and therefore nomi-
nally supporters of the Imperial cause.

Our picturesque protectors pause every now and then,
peering anxiously toward the south, suspicious of every dot
on the horizon, of every patch that seems to move in the
distance upon that sea of heat-waves that rolls above the
plain.   Most of our guards are young men under twenty-five,
one only is older.   Even sterner than the rest in aspect, he
has a cruel face, thick lips, and
wears a gray skull-cap drawn
tightly above his furrowed
forehead. We might well
have some misgivings for
our safety were not our
guards also our hosts, and
answerable for us to their
chief, who is answerable
to the Sultan.   Should
we suffer harm, the cen-
tral government must make
amends to the United States.

"EVEN STERNER THAN THE REST"

THE CARAVAN ARRIVES AT SUNSET

As if in preparation for the expected fray, the horsemen are continually rehearsing sham battles, half the troop dashing furiously ahead, then returning at full gallop to attack the caravan, which is stoutly defended by the other half. At

TENT OF THE WOUNDED TRIBESMAN

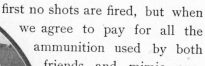

BERBER BELLES

first no shots are fired, but when we agree to pay for all the ammunition used by both friends and mimic enemies, blank charges are rammed into the elaborate old flintlocks, and the roar and smoke of harmless battle mark our advance into a hostile territory.

At sunset we arrive at Twazit. We expected to find a village. We find instead a circle of thirty-six Bedouin tents pitched in the open plain. The men of our escort are here at home, and are greeted by their wives who ask for news of the chief and the rest of the troop. The women wring their hands and weep on learning that we are to camp with them. The reason is that should we be robbed while under the protection of their chief, the Sultan's government would hold their husbands responsible for all damages, and bleed even the poorest of them to repay us for our losses.

SIMPLE AS CHILDREN

An atmosphere of anxiety pervades the village. One man was killed in the morning's battle; he has just been hastily buried. Another is lying wounded in his tent, and we are urged to go to his relief; for every foreigner is supposed to be skilled in surgery and medicine. We are conducted to a low tent in which the wounded man is lying. He is surrounded by a stupid crowd, which keeps away fresh air. We

"WE EVEN DO A LITTLE VETERINARY SURGERY

strive to clear the tent, but curiosity is strong, and a score of villagers insist on witnessing the doctor's visit. The man lies on a rug groaning in fever, his garments stained with blood. His wound is red with clotted blood. No one has thought to wash him and give him water. My friend puts cooling bandages upon his head, and to the best of his ability dresses the wound. It is ugly, but not fatal; for the ball has glanced along the ribs and passed out on the side.

While I am striving to keep the crowd away, two women, smeared with slimy mud from head to foot, come running

SUSPICIOUS OF EVERY DOT ON THE HORIZON

THE OLD KAID PREPARES TO SALLY FORTH

from the river. They break into the tent, and throw themselves upon the prostrate form, uttering loud cries; and it is
with the greatest difficulty that we prevent those miserable
mud-daubed wives from overwhelming the sufferer with their
conventional expressions of grief. They have put on mud
and slime as substitutes for sackcloth and ashes.

BEYOND THE REACH OF DANGER

It is insisted that some medicine should be administered internally. "All doctors make sick people swallow medicine," they say ; and to conform to custom, and yet do no harm, we give our patient a cup of water in which a little paregoric has been dropped. Then, with a "Trust in Allah!" the foreign doctors retire amid the blessings of the crowd.

A PORTUGUESE PORTAL

Could we have cured but one tenth of the maladies, or in any small way relieved the needless suffering which greets the traveler in Morocco, we should have been happy ; but we were not prepared ; we lacked both knowledge and medical supplies. It grieved us to play the impostor, yet it was kinder to the people, who in many things are simple as children. To refuse them advice and treatment would have been cruel, however worthless the advice and treatment. Our willingness to serve our doses of paregoric, our injunctions to

"UP TO THE EYES IN DAISIES"

trust in the one God, pleased and cheered them. That was all that we could hope to accomplish.

We even do a little veterinary surgery for a wounded horse, a fine gray steed, lamed by a bullet in the leg. The poor beast is held prostrate while the bullet is cut out with my pocket-knife, and the wound is cauterized with red-hot iron. The excitement keeps us from a realizing sense of our situation, and it is only when in the gathering darkness

AN EMPTY TOWN

we have returned to our tent that we begin clearly to recognize the fact that these little scenes of such a painful interest are not prepared merely to amuse the curious traveler. There is a stern reality in it all ; and the Beni-Zimour who, this very morning, attacked the village and laid low men and horses, are not many miles away.

The night is clear. The few men in camp are constantly on the alert. We see the chief mount and ride outside that circle of flimsy tents, our only fortification. He goes to see that the patrols are not neglecting duty, to scan with anxious eyes the southern distance.

All is still till half-past nine. Then comes the most uncomfortable quarter of an hour that I have ever passed. A shrill, loud cry rings out ; we think it is the call to prayer. Not so ; it is the call to arms. " *Hayel!* "—" to horse," the sentinels have shouted ; and that cry of " *Hayel* " is answered by pandemonium in the village. The tribesmen

" WHERE THE SEBU MEETS THE SEA "

rush to loose their shackled steeds, a hundred cowardly dogs begin to bark, and from every tent women and children rush out terror-stricken and weeping.

Their cries, the tramp of hoofs, the guttural shouts of our wild-eyed protectors combine to wake us to a sense of personal danger. The sentinels have seen a moving mass upon the plain, supposedly a band of Zimour horsemen. They are in expectation of a prompt attack. Our troop hur-

SEAWARD FORTIFICATIONS — MEHEDIA

riedly assembled, sallies out to meet the coming foe. A troubled silence reigns.

We wait and wait. No sound ; no clash of arms ; no shots exchanged. Five, ten, twenty minutes pass, then comes tramp of hoofs, a dark mass sweeps into the vague circle of Bedouin tents, the dogs stop barking, and with relief we recognize our faithful cavaliers as they dismount, giving grunts of satisfaction.

The approaching enemy had been frightened off by the unexpected appearance of our little army. Their force was small, they had believed the village unprotected, and they did not know that the bravest Beni-Hasan men had returned to guard their women and their homes. The sentinels are doubled, and after an hour more of watching, we fall asleep, weary with the day's excitement.

And as, next day, our journey is peacefully resumed with a smaller escort than before, we are inclined to laugh at the terrors of the night, and to chaff one another on our respective preparations for defense or flight. My warlike friend had spent that anxious hour cleaning his shotgun, removing bird-shot from his shells, and substituting crude lumps of lead obtained from Kaid Lharbi's store of ammunition. I had quietly packed my photographic films into the smallest possible bundle, and gone to bed, ready at a moment's notice to seize the precious packet and escape—whither, I did not know.

ABANDONED PALACES

THE RIVER BU RAGREG NEAR RABAT

By midday on the morrow we are beyond the reach of harm. Making a small present to the Beni-Hasan guards, we watched them disappear in the direction of the seat of war, where they will continue their life of skirmish and pillage until laid low by bullets from their hated Zimour neighbors.

And as, some hours later, we approach the coast, our caravan plunges into a veritable ocean of freshness, where

THE STORKS OF MEHEDIA

the wild daisies are so tall that our animals appear to be lying down, while in reality they are toiling on as best they may through a sea of flowers four feet deep. Our pet mule, the little white one, is almost up to his eyes in daisies, while the others revenge themselves for many days of dry, short, withered grass by feasting upon the rich fare so unexpectedly encountered. For several miles we slowly advance along this curious road (for we are still upon a road, though one little used) and at last, reaching a hilltop, we are greeted by a glorious salt breeze, and looking westward we behold the dim blue stretches of the broad Atlantic.

An hour more and we arrive at Mehedia, formerly a city of the Portuguese, to-day a vast ruin in the midst of which a miserable Arab hamlet is concealed. We camp near the decaying walls, where storks and men, gifted with equal intelligence, observe us with a silent curiosity. This Mehedia was once a flourishing port, and the fortifications left by the Portuguese are very stately and must have been at one time thoroughly impregnable. To-day, however, everything is dilapidated and forsaken.

We descend to the beach and enjoy a dip in the salty waters where the River Sebu meets the sea. Above us loom the imposing walls and bastions of Mehedia, silent and abandoned, yet eloquent of the vanished glory of Portugal.

THE BASHA PROVES HIS PROWESS

A PART OF THE IMPERIAL HAREM

In the thought of this empty fortress, so formidable in aspect, so monumentally defenseless in its desolation, there is something almost awe-inspiring. Its few miserable human denizens seem like dejected ghosts gliding through the crumbling portals, haunting the roofless palaces. The stork population on the wall-tops and the battlements seems more real. The Moors declare, "Storks are men who have come from islands far away to

THE GREAT WALL OF SALLI

the west upon the great ocean to see Morocco.   Like
all the world they know there is no other land to compare with it ; they abandon their outward form of men, and
come hither to behold it.   Therefore we give them hospitality and do not harm them.''   Nay, the Moors do more

BEFORE ENTERING SALLI

than this for the long-legged dwellers on their house-tops —
they maintain in Fez a hospital for invalid storks, founded, so
runs the legend, in this wise : Several hundred years ago a
stork came to the Kadi of Fez bringing a pearl necklace that
it had stolen.   As the owner could not be found, with the pro-
ceeds from the sale of the necklace, the Kadi bought a house
that is still in existence, called the Stork House, an institution where storks are received and treated as human beings.*

* Budgett Meakin—" The Land of the Moors."   Mr. Meakin's three volumes, " The
Moorish Empire," " The Land of the Moors," and " The Moors" are recommended to
readers who desire fuller information concerning Morocco and its people.

RABAT

The Moorish lover looks upon the stork with a peculiar reverence and affection, for from its haunts on terrace or tower the bird looks down upon the habitations of the women, and daily beholds the beloved one. But storks of Mehedia take no more heed of us than do the gray-robed human inhabitants.

On the eve of our departure, the Kaid of the village cannot resist exhibiting his skill with a recently acquired Winchester rifle that, he tells us, has been taken from

ON THE BEACH AT SALLI

smugglers in the performance of his official duties. Learning that we are Americans and therefore compatriots of his new gun, he deigns to look with favor upon us and invites us to his dwelling. There he prepares to astonish us with his marksmanship. An egg is placed upon a wall fifty feet distant. The Kaid seats himself comfortably on a ledge, takes leisurely aim, amid the respectful silence of his followers, and then bangs away. The plaster on the wall was badly damaged, but after the smoke had cleared away, the egg, intact, looked down upon the humbled Moor, who proceeded to examine and criticise the sights of the Winchester.

THE RIVER BU RAGREG

My friend, when his turn came to try the gun, was not considerate enough to spare the egg. His pride in his marksmanship overcame his politeness, as a yellow blotch on that old wall may still attest.

From Mehedia it is one day's ride southward to the sister-cities of Salli and Rabat, sister-cities which have never been on the best of terms with one another. We follow a sandy trail along the coast — the monotony of the journey broken by but a single incident, an encounter with a gaily furnished caravan. Six Moorish women robed in white, with covered faces, attended by a dozen guards and servants, come slowly along the dusty track. At their approach Kaid Lharbi, evincing a sudden bashfulness, dashes off to the right, points his horse's head toward the sea, and sits there with his back turned to the veiled beauties until the gay parade has passed. The other men of our escort follow his example, galloping off to one side or the other, planting their steeds with tails toward the trail, not venturing to look around until the dust raised by the passing caravan has settled. We naturally seize our cameras to record this strange proceeding, whereupon they shout imperatively, "Turn your backs quickly! These are the Sultan's wives. No man may look upon them!" Accordingly we, too, conform to a custom which seems to us rude rather than courteous and turn our backs upon the mysterious beauties, a contingent of Imperial wives whom Mulai El-Hasan is shipping in advance to await his arrival at Mehedia or Mequinez.

A few hours later we pass beneath the aqueduct of Salli, which serves also as an outer city-wall. Then, after watering our animals, we ride on across vast vacant spaces until the gates of Salli admit us to the famous city of the old-time "Salli Rovers."

So hostile is the populace that every attempt at picture-making brings a volley of stones from howling urchins and threatening murmurs from savage-looking citizens. All that we remember of our visit to Salli is a rapid dash through narrow thoroughfares amid a sprinkling of missiles and male-dictions. It is with a sense of relief that we find ourselves on the broad sandy beach that stretches from the southern

SWITCHING THE " BAGGAGE-CAR "
AT THE FERRY

THE SALLI-RABAT FERRY

walls down to the River Bu Ragreg, on the opposite shore of which rises the city of Rabat, our destination. As we look back toward the white line traced by Salli's gleaming house-tops, our thoughts go back to the hero of our childhood, Robinson Crusoe who, taken by the Salli Rovers, was there held in slavery for many months, finally escaping in a small boat belonging to his Moorish master. Another famous char-acter, Captain John Smith, came to Salli in 1604; but why he came and what he did there we do not definitely know. For years the Corsairs of this port were the scourge of Chris-tian merchant-ships. Piracy was then a recognized profes-sion, the title "pirate" an honorable one, in fact, the highest naval title of to-day is but a corruption of that assumed by the old pirate chiefs: "Lord of the Sea," "Ameer-el-Bahr,"—Admiral!

Salli and Rabat, although within gunshot of one another, differ widely in character. Salli is rabidly anti-foreign.

Rabat is commercial and comparatively cordial to Christians, sheltering a little colony of European merchants and vice-consuls.

Between the cities flows the Bu Ragreg, "Father of Glittering," across which we must be ferried in crude flat-bottomed barges. To switch our baggage-train on to the ferry-boat is a task that calls for much hard work and not a little Arabic profanity.

We must wait our turn ; for there are other caravans, with camels, mules, and horses massed upon the sands. At last our animals are all embarked with the exception of Bokhurmur's burro, who, accustomed only to fording, requires much persuasion before he will trust himself to this new-fangled contrivance. During the brief period of calm that intervenes between the embarkation and subsequent landing on the Rabat beach, we look in admiration at the scene about us. Above the palisade on the south bank rises a noble half-completed tower. We have long since heard reports of it.

HIS FIRST EMBARKATION

RABAT — THE CITY AND THE CITADEL

It is the unfinished Hasan Tower, a sister to the famed
Giralda of Seville and to the Kutubiya of Morocco City.
The same Sultan, Yakub el Mansur, the great builder, reared
this trinity of towers about eight hundred years ago. To-
day they prove the vast extent of his dominion ; to him
owed allegiance all the lands which lie between Andalusia in
the south of Spain, and Marrakesh, on the borders of the
Great Sahara. But this tower at Rabat was never finished.
It stands to-day as the workmen left it in the year 1200.

Rabat owes its existence to the builder of the tower, who
late in the twelfth century founded on this promontory his
"Camp of Victory," "Rabat el Fatih." The frowning citadel sits darkly on the crest between the harbor and the sea,
the smiling city lies gleaming just below. We follow the
broad, animated beach, enter at the water-gate, present our
credentials to the governor, and after some delay a camping-
ground is assigned us on the crest within the shadow of the

citadel, under the very walls of the powder magazine. It is not until our outfit is here unpacked, that we remark the fact that we are pitching our tents in a graveyard. All round-about us are neglected graves, tombstones inclined at most distressing angles, with hollows where there should be mounds, and weeds and rubbish in place of grass and flowers.

Poor Abuktayer, sick from fatigue and bad water drunk on the journey, is excused from work, and sits amid the mossy mortuary tablets, a picture of weariness and woe, watching the other servants as they wedge tent-pegs into the cracks of tombstones.

Grewsome indeed our camping-ground, but good enough for Christian dogs, the amiable Basha thinks, and the Christian dogs have ceased to be fastidious. All that we ask is that the sleeping Moors, buried only two feet underground, will manifest toward us the same aloofness as is shown by their living co-religionists. But although

OUR CAMP AT THE RABAT POWDER HOUSE

our foreground is not cheerful to contemplate, the views in two directions are superb. Looking eastward we see the snow-white city with its "saint-houses" and minarets, and in the distance the square, commanding tower, high above the winding river. The seaward vista is not less attractive. The wide ocean stretches peacefully westward to the new world; at our feet the warlike pomp of the old world is displayed in the six

ABUKTAYÊR

stately camps of Bashas from the interior provinces. These Bashas have come to Rabat to greet the Sultan who, with his mighty caravan, is expected within a fortnight. Four thousand horsemen are assembled at Rabat to escort the Imperial train from Rabat to Fez. Every evening, just before sunset, fine old gentlemen in spotless robes of white toil up to our hill-top, and, passing our camp without a side glance or a salutation, spread small red rugs upon the tombs, seat themselves thereon, and watch the slow sun sink into the progressive west. Then in the twilight they rise, fold up

Photograph by Cavilla

THE HASAN TOWER—RABAT

their rugs, and with a measured tread return to the white city
whence they came.   Seven times we saw the same old
worthies come, watch, and depart, but never was there a
glance of recognition, never a sign they are conscious of our
presence amid the resting-places of their dead.   Therefore
we were surprised, one evening, when three dignified personages halted before our tents, spoke a few words to Haj, and

THE CAMPS OF THE GOVERNORS

then sat down on tombstones and began a serenade with a
violin, a tambourine, and a peculiar form of Oriental guitar.
A glance at their dress tells us that these men are Jews ; a
word of explanation from Haj tells us that they are sent to
play for us by the local Consular-Agent of the United States,
a native Jew, upon whom we had called the day before.

Among the European residents of this remote port is an
eccentric Englishman from Gibraltar who has built for himself in Rabat the tallest dwelling in Morocco, a house of four
stories, its façade conspicuous because of its unusual height

and its coat of bright blue paint.   On several occasions the
owner of this unique Moorish skyscraper entertained us at
dinner, and insisted that we should lodge under his aspiring
roof on stormy nights, when our camp was drenched with
rain.   In view of this cordial treatment extended to entire
strangers, we are surprised
to learn that our host is

MINSTRELS OF ISRAEL

not on speaking terms with other members of the foreign
colony.   That he lives practically alone, attended by an old
Spanish housekeeper.   In every corner of the world the traveler is sure to find the solitary Englishman dwelling in Anglo-
Saxon seclusion and independence amid strange peoples,
sufficient unto himself, his house his castle, his excuse for
self-banishment the remark, "Oh, I rather like the place,
you know; good air, fine climate."

Rabat is primarily a place of business; the markets and
bazaars are always thronged.   Rug-making is the industry
for which the port is noted, and every day we see itinerant
auctioneers, weighted down with brilliant carpets trudging

through the streets, calling the latest bid, and offering the fabric for the examination of would-be purchasers. Unfortunately, modern Rabat carpets, like Navajo blankets, have suffered from the introduction of aniline dyes. The colors are crude, the designs less artistic than in earlier times. The local industry, once carried to perfection, is fast degenerating, and Rabat rugs are no longer things of worth and beauty.

In all things the Moors have continually retrograded since the conquest of Granada. From one of the foremost, they have become almost the last of nations; their arts, their sciences, their industries forgotten, nothing remains to them save their skill in horsemanship, their bravery in battle, and their fixed belief in the predestination of all things, good or evil.

THE TALLEST HOUSE IN MOROCCO

A crazy saint replied when we reproached him for being drunk with rum, "It is no sin. It is written." Those fatalistic words, "It is written — God has willed it," have been the cause of Moorish retrogression. They have robbed the people of ambition and energy; the Moor, in time of disaster, shifts the responsibility upon Allah, and murmurs resignedly,

BUSINESS IN RABAT

"It is written." This philosophy helps him to bear the ills of life, great and small. For example, if a Moor chances to seat himself upon a tack, he does not curse nor swear nor rail at fate, nor does he wince as he withdraws the offending point. Far be it from him to protest. He simply murmurs, "It is written," and carefully replaces the tack for some other Moor to sit upon.

On the fifth morning of our sojourn in Rabat, we note a mighty stir in all the military camps within and roundabout the city. Mysterious moving statues appear upon the housetops to watch the passing of armed men through the streets. Troops of gorgeously arrayed horsemen gallop across the town, filling the narrow lanes and covered bazaars with clatter and confusion.   We ask the cause of all this sudden animation.   The answer is, "The Prince arrives to-day.   Our future Sultan, Abd-el-Aziz, is approaching from the south to herald the advance of his imperial father, Mulai El-Hasan III, who returns victorious from Tafilet and Tadla where he has chastised the revolted tribes and 'eaten up' rebellious provinces."   The Sultan had written to the waiting Bashas in words like these : "To you do I confide my best beloved son, my Mulai Abd-el-Aziz.   Receive, protect, and honor him as if he were myself and something more."   That "something more" bore a deep meaning, which was to be revealed within six days.

Rabat turns itself wrong-side-out to welcome the young prince.   The Bashas and Kaids, who, with their retinues, have been awaiting Imperial orders, now sally out from the south

ITINERANT AUCTIONEERS

RABAT RUGS

gates, followed by the entire population in festival attire.
We mount our horses, and with Haj and Kaid Lharbi as
escort join in this picturesque exodus.   An hour later we
find ourselves in the midst of an armed multitude, massed on
the hillsides stretching southward from the city walls and
overlooking the narrow plain along the sea-shore, which is to
be the avenue of approach for the princely caravan.   We are
the only white men in that vast expectant throng, the only
"Christian dogs" who have vent-
ured beyond the gates.   Haj
wears an anxious look ; he
knows that we are acting
rashly in thus exposing
ourselves unguarded to
the whims of an army
of fanatics.   But the
spectacle is worth the
risk.   Four thousand
cavaliers are assembled
along the crests of the hills

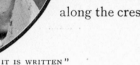

"IT IS WRITTEN"

GATE OF SHELLA

or in the plain below, where battle seems to rage, for
thence rises the smoke of oft-repeated volleys and the roar
of musketry. Troop after troop is there performing the
"powder play," Lab-el-Baroud, that very thrilling cavalry-
manœuver peculiar to the "rough riders" of the Arab race.

MYSTERIOUS MOVING STATUES ON THE HOUSE-TOPS

A dozen cavaliers advance in a broad platoon, first at
canter, then full gallop, then at a furious run, *ventre à terre*,
the horses at their highest speed, the men erect in the stirrups, spinning and tossing their glittering flintlocks, until, at
a word from the chief, triggers are drawn, and the troop van-
ishes into a cloud of smoke. When the smoke rolls away,
there are the panting horses thrown back on their haunches,
motionless as statues ; and then, before we can give vent to
our admiration, another troop comes thundering along,
another volley racks the ears and clouds the air, another

ALL HORSEMEN SALLY SOUTHWARD

tableau forms, and dissolves in drifting smoke, until it seems as if all the hosts of the Prophet were joining in a universal fantasia in honor of the young prince who some day will be Commander of the Faithful, successor to the Shareefian throne founded by the grandson of Mohammed.

A BASHA AND HIS TROOP AT REST

POWDER PLAY — READY!

Then, when the troops are weary, two horsemen more energetic than the rest dash furiously at one another and without colliding they exchange muskets and deftly, instantaneously, kiss each other on the cheek.

THE START

FIRE

HALT!

MULAI ABD-EL-AZIZ APPROACHING RABAT

Meantime a slow, silent, interminable caravan has been creeping along the shore. As far as the eye can reach in both directions, the shore is dotted with tiny moving spots, some red, some white, some brown, as if a tribe of giant ants were crawling northward toward Rabat. We see mules and camels laden to death, urged on by cruel drivers; we see the weary foot-soldiers dragging themselves along clad in a

THE ENDLESS LINE OF HORSEMEN

ragged suit of red and blue ; we see superb Moors in spotless white, dignitaries of the imperial household, attended by mounted guards and running servants.

Suddenly Haj exclaims, ''There is the prince!'' He points to a white-robed boy, superbly mounted, with an attendant walking at each stirrup. Behind him comes a litter borne by two mules in which young Abd-el-Aziz may

A FRAGMENT OF THE LIVING WALL OF MEN AND HORSES

repose when weary of the saddle. Then follows a broad platoon of the Imperial Guards, fierce negro cavaliers, the Bokharis, in whom alone, of all the army, the Sultan places perfect trust. Slowly the prince's train nears the waiting multitude. The four thousand horsemen on the hill-tops form in one grand line, and, as the future ruler of Morocco comes in view, that mighty rank of flesh and blood descends majestically to the plain like a foamy wave receding from a beach. No illustration can suggest the majesty of that spectacle. The endless line of white, so faint and dim, which undulates along the hillsides, is in reality the Moorish army drawn up in one unbroken rank, a living wall along which the son of Mulai El-Hasan is to pass, receiving homage from the troop of every Kaid and Basha. As far as we can see, the line, though curved and bent by the inequalities of the ground, is perfect, unbroken, the white, flowing garments of the horsemen looking like a mere thread lying along the slope and stretching away over the summit of a distant hill even to the city gates. As soon as the prince's train has passed us, we dash across its wake and ride along behind that wall of horsemen, peering through it at Abd-el-Aziz as he halts before each governor to receive the homage of the tribes. My one thought is to make a photograph of the prince during one of his brief pauses. Three times do I just miss my

UNIQUE PORTRAIT OF MULAI ABD-EL-AZIZ, EMPEROR OF MOROCCO

THE BASHA WITH HIS BANNERS AND BRIGADE

AS IN THE DAYS OF THE CRUSADES

THE SPECTACLE IS NOT FOR UNBELIEVERS

opportunity.   But at last, riding on in advance, I take
position directly behind two horsemen who appear like men
of prominence, and there await the passing of the imperial
youth.   As Abd-el-Aziz approaches, I am trembling with
excitement and anxiety; if I succeed, I shall have accom-

AWAITING THE IMPERIAL   ENTRY

plished what never be-
fore has been done ; if I
am detected in the act of
copying the features of
the sacred youth, the
consequences may be
serious — men have been
killed for lesser sacrilege.
The prince draws nearer ;
to my joy he halts di-
rectly before the men
who shield me from his
look.　Just as he draws
rein, the horses prance
apart and leave an open-
ing in the line.　Through
this gap the Prince looks

THE EMPEROR
ENTERS RABAT

wonderingly at me as I make a profound
salute, and at the same time level my camera, and
with a trembling finger press the button.　The click of the
shutter sends a cold chill through me.　I raise my hat and
bow a second time.　Abd-el-Aziz looks squarely at me, his
face impassive and expressionless.　He slightly inclines his
head.　Meantime the horsemen, with heads bent low, utter
in unison, with religious intonation, the words, "God bless
the days of our lord !"　"God send our lord victorious !"

These words should be spoken only to the Sultan ; but
has not Mulai El-Hasan commanded the Faithful to receive
his son, as if he were "myself and something more "?

The Prince is in appearance older than his age, being in
his fifteenth year.　In his mien there is a dignity beyond his
years　He looks the Sultan, and I recall the words of Haj :
"He may succeed his father before many months are past,
for rumor has it that El-Hasan III is hastening back to Fez to

die.'' Strange indeed that this thought should have come to me just then, for at the very moment that my eyes met those of Abd-el-Aziz, he was already Sultan —he was the Great Commander of the Faithful. The boy himself did not then know it ; the army and the people were still ignorant of the event ; but that very morning the old Emperor, Mulai El-Hasan III, had ''received the visit of death,'' and had closed his long career of mili-

A WOULD-BE CUSTOMER OF " WINCHESTER BROS."

tary journeyings. We therefore looked upon the face of one who almost within the hour had been called to rule the destinies of dark Moghreb, to sit on the Shareefian throne, to become the feared and hated ruler of a semi-barbarous land, to bear the Imperial burden of a direct descendant of Mohammed.

So absorbed are we in studying the face and manner of Abd-el-Aziz, that we forget our whereabouts, forget the

THE SULTAN'S BARGE AND THE ENTIRE MOORISH NAVY OF TO-DAY

thousands of horsemen who are chanting their welcome to the
son of their Emperor.   But when, a moment later, the Prince
rides on, we are suddenly aroused to a sense of our perilous
situation.   The troops which formed the left wing of the
host, and have already rendered their salute, have now
broken rank and come dashing northward behind the line of
cavaliers, that they may fall in at the upper end of the line

THE EMPEROR RETURNING FROM SALLI

and be at hand to take part in the final powder play as the
Prince enters the city gate.   A Basha, followed by his ban-
ner-bearers, advances toward us, his brigade forming a pha-
lanx so broad that we cannot hope to avoid its onrush.   To
the right escape is barred by the long file of white-robed
riders ; to the left we dare not ride, for another troop is there
racing past at full gallop.   We are hemmed in.   There is
nothing for it but to join in the tumultuous rush of the wave
of horses and men which is thundering toward us.   We

A PRINCELY RETINUE ON THE BEACH

urge our horses to their utmost speed, and a moment later we
find ourselves engaged in a race for safety, a roaring torrent
of Moorish warriors surging roundabout us. Should our
horses stumble, we are lost. No power on earth can stem
that furious tide. Our only salvation is coolly to guide our
running steeds, avoiding obstacles and collisions ; but how
easily an angered Moor, indignant at our having looked
squarely into the sacred countenance of his prince, could

SHIP AHOY ! BREAKING CAMP

ride us down, and attribute the accident to our rash attempt
to emulate the rough-riders of the Moroccan plains !

Thus we are swept onward as by the surge of a white-
crested wave, until the torrent breaks against the grim old
walls of Rabat, and the flood of horsemen recoils, divides,
and spreads itself on either side of the trail leading to a
massive medieval gate.

The scene recalls the days of the Crusades. An armed
host is at the gate of a walled city, fantastic banners wave,
the clash and roar of battle and the tramp of many hoofs is
heard, and then a mighty shout rings from six thousand
throats as the gate swings open to admit an Emperor's son.

The spectacle is not for unbelievers, but we have cautiously drawn near enough
to witness the triumphal
entry and to hear the shrill
salutations of the thou-
sand closely veiled
Moorish women who are
massed on either side
of the imposing portal.

Then follows a mad

REGRETS!

rush cityward of soldiers and civilians. The tortuous pas-
sages of the old gates are choked for hours with swirling
currents of humanity. By the time we have reached our
camp by a circuitous route, Abd-el-Aziz is safely housed in
the Imperial Palace of Rabat. The dying wish of Mulai
El-Hasan has been accomplished, his favorite son, and appointed successor, has reached in safety a fortified city, and
has been joined by a large and loyal force under the command of trusted chiefs. This has been done before the
elder son, or the ambitious uncle, has had time to learn of
Mulai El-Hasan's death, and to raise the standard of revolt.
Seldom it is that a Sultan mounts peacefully to his throne.
There are always many claimants, each supported by a
faction ; and had Hasan's death been known in Fez while
Abd-el-Aziz was on the road, he never would have had
a chance at the succession despite the expression of his
father's will.

On the day of his proclamation the young Sultan makes
a triumphal progress through the streets. He rides a superb
horse, with rich green trappings. His form is hid in folds of
white. On either side walks the Mul-es-Shuash, a trusted
retainer charged with the task of waving a cloth to flick
imaginary flies from the Imperial Master. The Sultan lacks,

however, the most important insignia of Moorish Majesty, the scarlet umbrella, which is now being carried across the southern plains in the funeral cortege of his father. Companies of red-clothed infantry guard the prince; he is followed by a hundred dignified Moors magnificently mounted. His passing is greeted with enthusiastic shouts from the men in the streets, and shrill piercing cries, of " You, you, you! " from hundreds of veiled women on the house-tops.

We follow the procession to the beach, and watch the Emperor embark on the Imperial barge, which will bear him to Salli to pray in one of the historic mosques. A short distance up the river the entire Moorish Navy lies at anchor — a solitary little steam-yacht, dressed with many flags, but too poor even to fire a salute. An hour later his Majesty returns and, joined by the princely retinue in waiting on the Rabat side, re-enters the city to confer with the viziers of his late father and make plans for a triumphal progress inland to Fez, his capital.

With intense interest we have followed these events; we are conspicuously unwelcome to the Moors, being forced into prominence in our efforts to attain effective points of view for making photo-  graphic records of these historic incidents. We wonder why we are not molested — why we are

THE FINAL " PACK-UP "

able to escape the stonings to which many a rash Christian on-
looker has been subjected.   Haj, the invaluable, makes clear
the reason of our immunity.   Knowing that our actions would
make us objects of hostility, the ingenious Haj spent several
days, before the arrival of the Prince, in visiting the numerous
military camps and spreading among the Bashas, Kaids, and

THE SULTAN AND HIS FLY-FLICKERS

Sheiks, certain reports concerning us and the object of our
presence, that would insure our safety and give us a high
place in the estimation of every warlike Moor.

The Moors admire above all things a good gun.   To them
the repeating Winchester is the noblest work of man.
The tribesman armed with one of those coveted American
weapons is worth a dozen enemies armed with the native
flintlock.   Therefore did Haj conceive a fabrication that
worthily crowned the forty days of persistent perjury to
which we owed so many splendid opportunities.   Discreetly,
confidentially, he informed the men of every tribe that we,

his Christian masters, were no less personages than the "Winchester Brothers," makers of the famous rifles, proprietors of the vast factories in America. We are come, he added, to perfect plans for arming the tribes faithful to the Emperor, that they may quickly exterminate the rebellious Beni-Zimour and the other unsubdued clans which defy the Imperial power. And the chieftains said to Haj, "As God is great, we shall protect your

INTERESTED

noble masters! They may move as freely as they wish amidst our troops, who will treat them with due respect." During our last days in Rabat, obsequious warriors came to our camp bringing broken Winchesters, begging us to repair them. One morning a handsomely-mounted boy, the son of a powerful Kaid, rode up attended by a small escort. He asked for Mr. Winchester. My friend bowed low and blushed. The little fellow kissed his own hand, my friend did likewise. Then, through our interpreter, the boy placed an order for a boy's-size Winchester, instructing us to make the best rifle that money could buy, very light and small, but large enough to kill sixteen rebels without reloading. We entered the order on the seared and yellow pages of our Christian consciences. Our fame as fabricants of arms threatened to get us into trouble ; inquiries and demands for repairs increased each day. We were not sorry when, a few days later, our summons to depart was given by the whistle

of a coasting merchant-ship which loomed up off the bar, as
the fog lifted shortly after sunrise.

The order to break camp is given ; our men work with a
will, for should we fail to reach the ship in time, it will mean

READY FOR THE BATTLE WITH THE BREAKERS

a delay of at least two weeks or a long land-journey with the
animals, along the sandy coast road to Tangier. We bid
farewell to Achmedo, Kaid Lharbi, Abuktayer, and Bokhurmur, to the horses, mules, and burros, which are to find their
way slowly back to Tangier by land, while we, with Haj and
remaining provisions, go cruising up the coast in comfort on
an English ship.

Embarkation at Rabat is easier to plan than to accomplish. No ship can cross the bar ; if the wind blows from
the west, the huge native lighters cannot climb over the
inrolling breakers, and the ship, after a courteous delay,
steams off, leaving the drenched, discomfited passengers to
return shoreward and possess their souls in patience until
there comes the happy conjunction of a passing steamer and
a calmer day.

Fortune, however, favored us in this as it did in all other things during our wanderings in Morocco. True, the breakers are rolling mountain-high across the bar, the forty-foot lighter is tossed like an egg-shell on their crests, or dropped with awful suddenness into abysses formed between cliffs of green transparent water. But our sturdy crew of twenty Salli men, descendants of the famous Rovers, attack the billows with that dogged perseverance that made their fathers the masters of the sea and all that sailed upon it. Wave after wave sweeps past — green-robed, with draperies foaming

FAREWELL!

white, as if the cohorts of the sea were striving to surpass the Moorish squadrons in a glorious lab-el-baroud — a
powder play where foam and spray and the roar of waters
supplant the flowing burnooses, rolling smoke, and din of
volley firing.

This is our last impression of Morocco, this overwhelming "fantasia" of the billows.   And as we look back
through clouds of flying spray at the grim Kasbah of Rabat,
at the white city, and the smiling hillsides roundabout, we
say with Pierre Loti, "Farewell, dark Moghreb, Empire of
the Moors, mayst thou remain, many years yet, immured,
impenetrable to the things that are new ! Turn thy back
upon Europe ! Let thy sleep be the sleep of centuries, and
so continue thine ancient dream.   And may Allah preserve to
the Sultan his unsubdued territories and his waste places carpeted with flowers, there to do battle as in old times the
Paladins, and gather in his harvest of rebel heads ! May
Allah preserve to the Arab race its mystic dreams, its immutability scornful of all things, and its gray rags ; may he preserve to the Moorish   ruins their shrouds
of whitewash, and   to the mosques
their inviolable   mystery !"

BATTLING WITH THE BREAKERS